A Student's Guide to History

A Student's Guide to History

Jules R. Benjamin

ST. MARTIN'S PRESS · New York

For Elaine

907.2
B 468 a
1975

Preface:
To the Student

The aim of this book is to introduce you to the study of history and to assist you in history courses. Whether you are studying World History, Western Civilization, Ancient History, Modern History, European History, United States History, or another historical subject, this volume will present some basic concepts and methods of the field and help you acquire the skills you will need in your work.

The first chapter discusses the purposes and uses of historical study and how historians investigate their subjects. Chapters 2 and 3 explain how to read a history assignment, give a classroom talk, and organize and write a book report or essay exam. In the fourth and fifth chapters the book treats a more complex matter, how to prepare and write a research paper; these chapters will help you choose a topic, use the library to gather information, organize your research, and

99157

present the results of your work in your paper. The appendixes contain reference sources and general information that you will find useful both in your present course and in any other history courses you may take later on.

Throughout the book it should be clear that the study of history is not an idle journey into a dead past, but an aid to understanding and living in the present. The basic ideas and tools introduced here should help you make use of history to answer important questions about your own life and your relationship to the world. This use, in the end, is what makes history valuable.

J. R. B.

Contents

chapter 1

The Subject of History and How to Use It

What Historians Are Trying to Do

Since the time when human beings invented writing, they have left records of their understanding of the world and of the events in their lives and how they felt about them. By studying the records that previous generations have left, we can find out about the kind of lives they led and how they faced their problems. We can use what we learn about the experiences of people who lived before us to help solve problems we face today. Though the modern world is quite different from the societies in which our ancestors lived, the story of their accomplishments and failures is the only yardstick by which we can measure the quality of our own lives and the success of our social arrangements.

All of us look into the past from time to time. We read historical novels or books about historical events. We gaze at old photographs or listen to the stories our grandparents tell. Historians, however, make a serious and systematic study of the past and attempt to use the knowledge they gain to help explain human nature and contemporary affairs. Professional historians spend their lives pursuing the meaning of the past for the present. To amateurs, historical research is like a hobby, but their occasional journeys into the past may contribute to the store of human knowledge and can greatly influence their own lives. Your study and research as a student qualifies you as an amateur historian. Your study of the past is part of the same search for knowledge carried on generation after generation.

What History Can Tell You

Everything that exists in the present has come out of the past, and no matter how new and unique it seems to be, it carries some of the past with it. The latest hit recording by the newest group is the result of the evolution of that group's musical style and of the trends in music and society that have influenced them. Perhaps their style developed from earlier rock styles associated with the Beatles, or perhaps they are taking off from even older folk themes used by Bob Dylan. Well, Dylan was influenced by Woodie Guthrie, who wrote his songs in the 1930s and whose music grew out of his contact with the heritage of American folk music from the nineteenth century, which in turn had come in great measure from earlier music in England and Scotland, some of which has its origins in the Middle Ages. So you can see that the house of the present is filled with windows into the past.

The car you ride in, although it may have been designed only a few years ago, carries within it the basic components of the "horseless carriage" of the turn of the century. Your car works because people who knew how to make carriages, bicycles, and engines put their ideas together in a new way. The knowledge necessary to make the carriages and bicycles came, in turn, from earlier inventions. Some, like the wheel, go back into the antiquity of human history.

Everything has a history. At least part of the answer to any question about the contemporary world can come from studying the circumstances that led up to it. The problem is to find those past events, forces, arrangements, ideas, or facts that had the greatest influence on the present subject you have questions about. The more you understand about these past influences, the more you will know about the present subject to which they are related.

History and the Everyday World

Most of us are curious. Children are always asking their parents the "why" of things. When we grow up we continue to ask questions because we retain our fascination with the mysteriousness and complexity of the world. Because everything has a history, most questions can be answered, at least in part, by historical investigation.

What are some of the things about which you are curious? Have you ever wondered why women's skirts in old movies are so long, or why Frenchmen often embrace one another whereas Englishmen almost never do? Perhaps you have wondered how the Kennedy or Rockefeller families came to be rich, or why the Japanese attacked Pearl Harbor. Have you thought about why most of the peoples of southern Europe are Catholic whereas most northern Europeans are not? Many oriental peoples bow when they greet one another; we shake hands. The questions could go on forever; all the answers are written somewhere in the record of the past.

The record of the past is not only contained in musty volumes on library shelves; it is all around us in museums, historical preservations, and the antique furnishings and utensils contained in almost every household. Our minds are living museums because the ideas we hold (for example, democracy, freedom, equality, competitiveness) have come down to us by way of a long historical journey. Though we are usually unaware of it, the past is always with us. Because history is literally at our fingertips, we can travel back into it without difficulty.

A Brief Journey into the Past

If you have ever driven any distance, you have probably ridden over a system of very modern superhighways with high speed limits and no cross traffic or stoplights. This national highway network, built within the last fifteen years, connects all the major United States cities and is known as the interstate system. These roads were planned by the Eisenhower Administration in 1955, and, though they are the newest highways in the country, they have a history two decades long.

Looking for the marks of history in the world around us is something like the task of the geologist or archeologist. However, instead of digging down into the earth to uncover the past, the historical researcher digs into the visible, everyday elements of society to find the historical roots from which they sprang. The fact that the interstate highway system built in the 1960s and 1970s had its origins in the 1950s is just, so to speak, the uppermost layer of history. If a study of the newest highways can take us back twenty years, what about the historical roots of the older highways or of the country roads? How far into the past can we travel on them?

Turn off the eight-lane interstate, past the gleaming Exxon station, past the orange roof of the Howard Johnson restaurant, past the bright signs before the multistoried Holiday Inn, and onto, say, U.S. Route 51 or 66. These are older highways, built mostly in the 1940s and 1950s. Being from an earlier period, like older strata of rock, perhaps they can tell us something of life in an earlier period of America.

When you leave the interstate system for this older road network you first notice that the speed limit is lower and that many of the buildings are older. As you ride along at the slower pace there are no signs saying "Downtown Freeway ½ mile" or "Indiana Turnpike—Exit 26N." They say "Lubbock 38 miles," or "Cedar Rapids 14 miles." As you approach Lubbock or Cedar Rapids, you will see motels less elaborate than the Holiday Inn. They may be small wooden cottages with fading paint and perhaps a sign that says "Star Motor Court" or "Stark's Tourist Cabins." Instead of Howard Johnson's or McDonald's, you may pass "Betty's Restaurant" or "Little River Diner." If you pay close attention to these buildings and do not become distracted by the more modern structures between them, you can take a trip into history even as you ride along. All of the older restaurants, stores, and gas stations you see were built before the large shopping centers and parking lots that separate them, and they are clues to the history of the highway on which you are riding. Places like the Star Motor Court and the Little River Diner probably were built when the road was new. Unless they have been modernized, they are relics of a previous historical period—when men named Roosevelt and Truman were president and when the cars that rode by looked like balloons with their big rounded hoods, trunks, and fenders. The diner isn't air-conditioned, and the sign over the tourist cabins proudly proclaims that they are "heated." This is the world of the 1930s and 1940s.

Now turn off the highway at State Route 104 where the sign says "Russell Springs 3 miles" or where it says "Hughesville 6 miles." Again the speed limit drops, and the bright colors fade further away. You are on a road that may have been built in the 1920s or 1930s or earlier (in older sections of America the country roads can go back a hundred years or more). Time has removed many of the buildings that once stood along this road, but if you look closely, the past is there ready to speak to you. The gas station here has only one set of pumps, and the station office sells bread, eggs, and kerosene. The faded advertisements on the wall display some products that you have never heard of—NeHi Orange and Red Man Chewing Tobacco. If you see a restaurant or motel, it may be boarded up because the people who used to stop in on their way to Russell Springs of Hughesville now go another way or may no longer live in the country but in a nearby city. However, many of the homes along Route 104 are still there. They were built when only farmland straddled the road, and they may go back to a time when horses and not internal combustion engines pulled the traffic past the front door. Such relics of early technology as old washing machines and refrigerators may stand on the tilting wooden porches, and a close look behind the tall weeds beside the dirt driveway may reveal the remains of a 1936 La Salle. As you stop before one of the old farmhouses, the past is all around you, and, although the place does not appear in its youthful form, a little imagination can reconstruct what life was like here on the day in 1933 when Roosevelt closed all the banks or the day in 1918 when the Great War in Europe ended.

The line linking past to present never breaks, and the house itself has a history, as do the people who once lived in it. In this sense, every house is haunted with its own past, and a keen eye can see the signs. Enter the house and you can see the stairway that was rebuilt in 1894, and the fireplace in the main bedroom upstairs, which was put in about 1878, the year the house was built. Perhaps the old Bible on the table near the bed notes the year the family came to the United States, and the dates in the early nineteenth century when the parents of the immigrants who built the house were born.

The story could go on forever, although the evidence would become slimmer and slimmer. You could find out from county records who owned the land before the house was built, going back perhaps to the time when the people who lived on the land were red, not white. In distance you may have traveled only ten or twenty miles from the interstate highway and it may have taken you less than an hour, but by looking for the signs of the past in the present, you have traveled a hundred years or more into history.

If you think and study about the passage of time between the old farmhouse on the country road and the gleaming service station by the interstate, you may come to understand some of the social, political, and economic forces that moved events away from the old wooden porch and sent them speeding down the interstate highway. The more you know about this process, the more you will learn about the times when the farmhouse was new and the more you will understand how the interstate highway came about, what you are doing riding on it, and into what kind of a future you may be heading.

Historians don't usually wander into history in such a casual fashion. They have to be trained in their methods of investigation and analysis. As an introduction to your own historical research and study, the next section will describe some of the tools employed by historians in their examination of the records of the past.

How Historians Work

Like you, historians are challenged by the complexity of the world, and many want to use their studies of the past to help solve the problems of the present. The questions that can come to mind are numberless, and serious historical investigators must choose wisely among them. They do not want to spend a lot of effort pursuing the kind of question to which history has no answer (for example, "What is the purpose of the Universe?" "Am I a lovable person?" "Who is the smartest person in the world?"). Nor do they want to struggle to achieve the solution to a problem that is not of real importance. (Historical investigation can probably tell you who wore the first pair of pants with a zipper in it, but that might not be worth knowing.) The main difficulty facing historians is not eliminating unanswerable or unimportant questions, but choosing among the important ones.

A historian's choice among important questions is determined by personal values, by the concerns of those who support the historian's work, by the nature of the time in which the historian lives, or by a combination of all of these. The ways in which these influences operate are very complex, and often historians themselves are unaware of them.

Historians investigate the questions they choose to study in many ways. Their particular approach depends on their academic training and their belief about which aspects of human nature and the human environment are most important to an understanding of their subject. Traditionally, historians have been divided into those who saw social, cultural, intellectual, political, diplomatic, economic, or psychological matters as central to answering the question being investigated. The social historian investigates the development of human groups and communities and their interaction with the larger society in which they emerge. The cultural and intellectual historian deals with the meaning of ideas and attitudes and their effect upon social changes. The political historian focuses on the operation and acts of governments, parties, and institutions, whereas diplomatic historians deal with relations between governments. The economic historian studies developments in technology, production, consumption, and the division of wealth. Most recently, a group known as psychohistorians have centered their investigations on the emotional development of individuals and families.[1]

When the historian has chosen his or her subject, many

---

[1] Historians also have been divided according to their particular *philosophies* of history. These are complex systems that try to explain the larger course and meaning of history. If you wish to look into this question, seek advice from your instructor.

questions still remain. For example, does historical evidence dealing with the subject exist, and if so, where can it be found? If someone wanted to study gypsy music from medieval Europe, and that music was never written down or mentioned in historical accounts of the period, then little or nothing can be found about this subject through historical research. Even if records exist on a particular subject, the historian may be unaware of them or unable to locate them. Perhaps the records are in an unfamiliar language or are in the possession of individuals or governments that deny access to them. Sometimes locating historical evidence can be a problem.

Having determined that records *do* exist and that they can be located and used, the historian faces another and more important problem: What is the credibility or reliability of the evidence? Is it genuine? How accurate are the records, and what biases were held by those who wrote them? If sources of information are in conflict, which is correct? Or is it possible that most of the sources are in error? Historians must pick and choose among the sources they uncover, and that is not always easy to do. The historian's own biases, as well, cloud the picture, making impartial judgment extremely difficult.

There are two basic forms of historical evidence: primary and secondary. Primary evidence records the actual words of someone who participated in or witnessed the events described. These can be newspaper accounts, diaries, notebooks, letters, minutes, interviews, and any works written (or otherwise recorded, as in photographs) by persons who claim first-hand knowledge of an event. Another primary source is official statements by established organizations or significant personages—royal decrees, church edicts, political party platforms, laws, and speeches.

Secondary evidence records the findings of someone who did not observe the event but who investigated primary evidence. Most history books fall into this category, although some are actually tertiary evidence because they rely not on primary evidence but are themselves drawn from secondary sources. When your own history research paper is finished, it will be secondary, or more likely, tertiary evidence to anyone who may use it in the future.

The problem of determining the reliability of evidence is a

serious one. Secondary and even primary evidence can be fraudulent, inaccurate, or biased. Eyewitness accounts may be purposely distorted in order to avert blame or to bestow praise on a particular individual or group. Without intending to misinform, even on-the-scene judgments can be incorrect. Sometimes, the closer you are to an event, the more emotionally involved you are, and this distorts your understanding of it. We can all recall events in which we completely misunderstood the feelings, actions, and even words of another person. Historians have to weigh evidence carefully to see if those who participated in an event understood it well enough to have accurately described it, and whether later authors understood the meaning of the primary documents they used. Official statements present another problem—that of propaganda or concealment. A government, group, or institution may make statements that it wishes others to believe, but that are not true. What a group says may not be what it does. This is especially true in politics.

To check the reliability of evidence, historians use the tests of consistency and corroboration: Does the evidence contradict itself and does it agree with evidence from other sources? Historical research always involves checking one source against another.

The bias of a source also presents difficulties. People's attitudes toward the world influence the way they interpret events. For example, you and your parents may have different attitudes toward music, sex, religion, or politics. These differences can cause you to disagree with them about the value of a rock concert, a Sunday sermon, or the president. Historians have their own attitudes toward the subjects they are investigating, and these cause them to draw different conclusions about the character and importance of religious, political, intellectual, and other movements. Later historians must take these biases into account when weighing the reliability of evidence.

In analyzing the evidence, the historian must find some way of organizing it so that he or she can make clear its meaning. A mass of facts and opinions concerning a subject is not a historical study. The task of the trained historian is to arrange the material so that it supports a particular conclusion. This conclusion may have been in the historian's mind at the outset, or it might be the result of investigation. If the evidence does not appear to support the conclusion, however, then the historian must either change that conclusion or seek other evidence to support it.

Once a historian is satisfied that research has uncovered sufficient evidence to support a particular conclusion, then he or she works to display the evidence in a manner that will clearly show that the conclusion drawn is a proper one. If any evidence that leads to other conclusions is uncovered, the historian has a responsibility to include it. In doing so, he or she must show how the supporting evidence is stronger than the nonsupporting evidence. There are many ways of organizing evidence in support of a conclusion. The historian's arguments in favor of a particular conclusion must be strong and convincing, and the logic of these arguments must not be faulty.

Recently, in an effort to eliminate error, bias, and faulty logic as much as possible, some historians have turned to techniques from mathematics and science to handle historical evidence and test conclusions. These historians prefer to deal with quantitative or uniform data that are easily comparable and that can be interpreted by mathematical formulas. Such researchers often use computers to analyze their data. They question historical findings involving opinion and judgment and look to types of evidence (usually statistical) that can test the more intuitive conclusions of other historians. The kinds of problems they deal with are usually narrow, and they have to be well trained in techniques of statistical analysis. Their tests of evidence are sophisticated and are becoming more so. The extent to which the study of history can or should become "scientific" is an important current debate among historians. (For some sources on quantitative historical data see Appendix A, section 8.)

chapter 2

How to Read a History Assignment and Take Notes in Class

How to Read a History Assignment

A common history assignment is the reading of a textbook. The best procedure for tackling the text is to *read* it. Many students hope to get by with their lecture notes, and they put off reading the text until just before the final exam. Reading the text week by week will give you the background knowledge necessary to understand the lectures and supplementary readings. In most courses the lectures embellish portions of the text, and lecturers assume that students are familiar with it. Sitting through a lecture on the economic aspects of the American Revolution will be confusing if you have not read the textbook discussion of the mercantilist theories behind many of the colonists' grievances.

Read the text chapters in close conjunction with the lectures to which they are related. Note the most prominent fac-

tual information and underline it. Also underline important
generalizations, interpretations, and conclusions. Don't skip
maps, charts, or diagrams. You are urged not to mark up
library books, but the reverse is recommended for books that
you own. Almost every page of the book should have some
underlining on it. But don't stop there. When you come across
a passage that makes an important point, illustrates the author's
values, or contains statements with which you disagree, write
your reaction or a summary of the passage in the margin. All
of this will come in handy when you prepare to take a test.
You will be able to reread the underlined material and your
comments and obtain a quick review of the chapter's contents.
Before the final, however, you may need to reread the text
itself, especially if you are having difficulty in the course or
wish to write an outstanding exam.

Another typical reading assignment is a historical novel or a
monograph (a specialized history work on a particular subject). In addition to the procedures used in reading a textbook,
you will need to pay special attention to the theme and point
of view of these works. They should be read more carefully
because your teacher will expect you to learn not only about
the subject they deal with, but about the emphasis and methods
of the work. Therefore, you will need to determine the author's
assumptions and values, and to understand the book's thesis
and conclusions. Read this kind of work not only to absorb the
facts, but also to analyze, question, and criticize. If you own
the book, you can do your questioning and criticizing in the
margins. If the book is not yours, make your remarks on
paper, and also write down a brief outline of the contents.
Then you can review your notes or underlinings before the
exam instead of rereading the entire book.

Some courses also involve the assignment of a book of
readings. These are usually a series of short essays (excerpts
from larger works or from primary documents) that deal with
a single subject. All of the suggestions concerning the reading
of texts and history books apply here as well, but this type of
assignment often calls for a particular kind of reading. Each
excerpt usually discusses a different aspect or interpretation of
the subject, and some are in serious disagreement. Teachers
expect students to be able to assess the arguments of the var-

ious writers and on occasion to take a position in the controversy. Therefore, you must read this particular kind of book with an eye to analyzing the arguments of the different excerpts or to comparing their different approaches to the subject. A good way to do this is to briefly summarize the argument or approach of each selection.

To help you appreciate the differences among the three types of reading assignments, here are passages from each. All of the works are histories of the Cold War, and the selection chosen from each concerns President Truman's 1947 speech to Congress, in which he called for a $400 million military and economic program of aid to anti-Communist forces in Greece and Turkey. In the speech the president also advocated that the United States act to oppose Communist movements throughout the world. This idea became known as the Truman Doctrine. As you read these passages, take note of the different manner in which each deals with this subject.

Textbook

The day before, 6 March, Truman had begun to prepare the ground. In a speech at Baylor University in Texas he explained that freedom was more important than peace and that freedom of worship and speech were dependent on freedom of enterprise. . . .

The State Department, meanwhile, was preparing a message for Truman to deliver to the full Congress. He was unhappy with the early drafts, for "I wanted no hedging in this speech. This was America's answer to the surge of expansion of Communist tyranny. It had to be clear and free of hesitation or double talk." Truman told Acheson to have the speech toughened, simplified, and expanded to cover more than just Greece and Turkey. He then made further revisions in the new draft. . . .

At 1 P.M. on 12 March 1947, Truman stepped to the rostrum in the hall of the House of Representatives to address the joint session of the Congress. The speech was also carried on nationwide radio. He asked for immediate aid for Greece and

Turkey, then explained the reasoning. "I believe that it must be the policy of the United States to support free peoples who are resisting attempted subjugation by armed minorities or by outside pressures."

The statement was all-encompassing. In a single sentence, Truman had defined American policy for the next twenty years. Whenever and wherever an anti-Communist government was threatened, by indigenous insurgents, foreign invasion, or even diplomatic pressure (as with Turkey), the United States would supply political, economic, and most of all military aid. The Truman Doctrine came close to shutting the door against any revolution, since the terms "free peoples" and "anti-Communist" were assumed to be synonymous. All the Greek government, or any dictatorship, had to do to get American aid was to claim that its opponents were Communists. And the aid would be unilateral, as Truman never mentioned the United Nations, whose commission to investigate what was actually happening in Greece had not completed its study or made a report.

Monograph

What was really on the mind of the president and his advisers was stated less in the Truman Doctrine speech than in private memos and in Truman's March 6 address at Baylor University. Dealing with the world economic structure, the president attacked state-regulated trade, tariffs, and exchange controls —". . . the direction in which much of the world is headed at the present time." "If this trend is not reversed," he warned, ". . . the United States will be under pressure, sooner or later, to use these same devices in the fight for markets and for raw materials. . . . It is not the American way. It is not the way to peace." [16] . . .

The question of how best to sell the new crusade perplexed the administration, not the least because

Greece was a paltry excuse for a vast undertaking of which it "was only a beginning," and in the end it formulated diverse reasons as the need required.[18] The many drafts that were drawn up before the final Truman Doctrine speech was delivered to Congress on March 12 are interesting in that they reveal more accurately than the speech itself the true concerns of Washington. Members of the cabinet and other top officials who considered the matter before the twelfth understood very clearly that the United States was now defining a strategy and budget appropriate to its new global commitments—interests that the collapse of British power had made even more exclusively American—and that far greater involvement in other countries was now pending at least on the economic level.

Quite apart from the belligerent tone of the drafts were the references to ". . . a world-wide trend away from the system of free enterprise toward state-controlled economies," which the State Department's speech writers thought "gravely threatened" American interests. No less significant was the mention of the "great natural resources" of the Middle East at stake.

Readings (excerpt from speech)

The very existence of the Greek state is today threatened by the terrorist activities of several thousand armed men, led by Communists, who defy the government's authority at a number of points, particularly along the northern boundaries. . . .

Meanwhile, the Greek Government is unable to cope with the situation. The Greek army is small and poorly equipped. It needs supplies and equipment if it is to restore authority to the government throughout Greek territory.

Greece must have assistance if it is to become a self-supporting and self-respecting democracy.

The United States must supply this assistance. . . .

At the present moment in world history nearly every nation must choose between alternative ways of life. The choice is too often not a free one.

One way of life is based upon the will of the majority, and is distinguished by free institutions, representative government, free elections, guarantees of individual liberty, freedom of speech and religion, and freedom from political oppression.

The second way of life is based upon the will of a minority forcibly imposed upon the majority. It relies upon terror and oppression, a controlled press and radio, fixed elections, and the suppression of personal freedoms.

I believe that it must be the policy of the United States to support free peoples who are resisting attempted subjugation by armed minorities or by outside pressures. . . .

It is necessary only to glance at a map to realize that the survival and integrity of the Greek nation are of grave importance in a much wider situation. If Greece should fall under the control of an armed minority, the effect upon its neighbor, Turkey, would be immediate and serious. Confusion and disorder might well spread throughout the entire Middle East.

Moreover, the disappearance of Greece as an independent state would have a profound effect upon those countries in Europe whose peoples are struggling against great difficulties to maintain their freedoms and their independence while they repair the damages of war. . . .

The free peoples of the world look to us for support in maintaining their freedoms.

If we falter in our leadership, we may endanger the peace of the world—and we shall surely endanger the welfare of this Nation.

Great responsibilities have been placed upon us by the swift movement of events.

I am confident that the Congress will face these responsibilities squarely.

Note that the textbook is general in its coverage. It does not use footnotes or quote from primary sources other than Truman's speech. It tries to summarize the content and meaning of the event without too much detail and without extensive proof for its conclusions. The monograph, on the other hand, covers a smaller portion of the topic, but it gives more detail, quotes from primary materials, and uses footnotes to record its sources of information. The selection from the book of readings is a primary source—the Truman speech itself. Often these books are composed of the original documents that form the basis of the historical events discussed by textbooks and monographs. Although this particular selection from a book of readings is a primary document, such works, as already noted, may also be collections of short essays or excerpts from monographs.

How to Take Notes in Class
The first rule concerning note-taking is simple: Pay attention. Don't sleep, doodle, talk, stare out the window, or write a letter to a friend. Some lecturers are not exactly spellbinding, but there is no point in going to class if you are not going to listen to the lecture.

Read the text before going to class or you may be taking notes on the material in the book. If everything the instructor says is new to you, you will spend so much time writing that you won't be able to get an understanding of the theme of the lecture. If you have obtained some basic information from outside readings you will be able to concentrate on noting points in the lecture that are new or different.

An instructor is most likely to prepare exam questions from material that he or she considers most important. It is therefore essential in preparing notes to determine which points in the lecture are given most prominent attention. Some instructors are very open about their preferences and clearly emphasize certain points, often writing them on the blackboard. Never fail to note something that the instructor indicates is important. Other instructors are less explicit about their biases and values, and you will have to try to figure them out. Listen closely, and make note of those interpretations and generalizations that seem to be stressed, especially when they differ from the approach in the text. You should not feel obliged to parrot your instructor's interpretations in an exam, but ignorance of them will work against you.

Your notes should be written legibly and headed by the date and subject of the lecture. They should reflect a general outline of the material covered, with emphasis on major interpretations and important facts not covered by the text. It is often best to write on every other line and to leave a large margin on at least one side of the page. This will allow you to add material later and to underline your notes and write marginal comments without cluttering the page.

If possible reread your notes later in the day on which they were written. If your handwriting is poor or your notes are disorganized, it is best to rewrite them. Check the spelling and definitions of any unfamiliar words, and be sure that the notes are coherent. Remember, your notes are an important source of information in your studies, and if they don't make sense you won't either.

To illustrate some of the essentials of good note-taking, here are portions of two sets of class notes taken from the same lecture. The first example illustrates many of the common errors of note-takers, and the second is an example of a well-written set of notes. The subject of the lecture was early European contact with Africa.

Example of Poor Note-Taking

Colonization of Africa—People were afraid to sail out. Afraid of sea monsters. But they liked the stories about gold in Africa. The Portuguese King Henry sailed south to find the gold mines and he built a fort at Elmina.

England and France want to trade with Africa. They begin trading. Competing with Portugal. These countries got into wars. They wanted to control Africa.

China had spices. They traded with Cairo and Venice. The Asians wanted gold, but the Islams stopped all trade. They fought wars about religion for hundreds of years. Fought over Jerusalem. The Pope called for a crusade. This was in the Middle Ages.

Spices came from Asia. In Europe they were valuable because the kings used them to become rich. They also ate them.

The Portuguese wanted to explore Africa and make a way to India. Their boats couldn't get around until Bartholemew Diaz discovered the Cape of Good Hope in 1487.

Most of all the Portuguese wanted slaves. They shipped them back from Africa. Columbus took them after he discovered America (1492). The Pope made a line in the Atlantic Ocean so the Catholics wouldn't fight. The colonies needed slaves. They sent 15 million from 1502 to the 19th century. Slaves did the hard work. They got free later after the Civil War.

Immigrants go to Africa from Europe but they don't like the hot weather and they catch diseases. The Dutch set up their own country at the Cape. Then the English conquer them.

Example of Good Note-Taking

Early European Contact with Africa   History 200
                                              10/22/75

I. Why did Europeans come to Africa?
  A. Desire for gold
    1. Medieval legends about gold in Africa.
    2. Prince Henry (Portuguese navigator) sent men down coast of Africa to find source of gold. (Also to gain direct access to gold trade controlled by Muslims.)
    3. Portuguese built forts along the coast. Their ships carried gold and ivory back to Portugal (16th century).
    4. Then the other Euorpean states came (England,

Holland, France, Spain) to set up their own
trading posts.

5. Competed with each other for African trade.
(Will talk about rivalry next week.)

B. Wanted to trade with Asia and weaken the Muslims
(The Muslims had created a large empire based
on the religion of Islam.)

1. Religious conflict between Christianity and Islam.
Fought a religious war in the 11th–12th centuries—
the Crusades.

2. The Muslims had expanded their empire when
Europe was weak. In 15th century they controlled
North Africa and they dominated trade in the
Mediterranean. They controlled the spices
coming from Asia, which were in great demand
in Europe. In Europe they were used to preserve
meat. So valuable, sometimes used as money.

3. Portugal and Spain were ruled by Catholic
monarchs. Very religious. The Catholic monarchs
wanted to force the Muslims out of Europe.
(They still held part of Spain.) Wanted to convert
them to Christianity.

I
M
P
O   }
R
T
A
N
T

4. The Muslims controlled North Africa and
Mediterranean trade. If the Portuguese and
Spanish could sail to the Indian Ocean directly
they could get goods from China and the Muslims
couldn't stop them. The way to Asia was the
sea-route around Africa.

C. The Europeans wanted slaves

1. When the Portuguese explored West Africa
(15th century) they sent back the first slaves
(around 1480).

2. The Spanish conquered the New World (Mexico,
Peru, etc.). (Columbus had made several trips
for the Queen of Spain.)

3. In America (the name for the New World)
they needed slaves. Most slaves were sent to
America.

4. Indians died from diseases of white men.
They were also killed in the wars. There was

I
M
P
O
R
T
A
N
T
} nobody to run the mines (gold and silver).
5. Sugar plantations of the Caribbean (and Brazil) needed labor. Cotton plantations in the south of U.S. also. It was hard work and nobody wanted to do it.
6. 15 million (maybe as many as 40 million) slaves were brought to work the plantations starting in 1502 until mid-19th century.

II. Colonization
   A. Immigration (why white people didn't come)
      1. They couldn't take the climate.
      2. There were a lot of tropical diseases.
      3. The Europeans didn't want to live in Africa, only run it.
      4. Only the Dutch settlers came. They set up the Boer states in South Africa. After them came British settlers.
      5. Frenchmen (some) settled in Algeria.
      6. Some English also moved to Rhodesia.
   B. Dividing Africa
      1. Whites began exploring into the interior. (Will discuss exploration next week.)

Copying notes during a lecture is difficult, and even a good set of notes can be greatly improved by being rewritten. Following is a rewriting of these notes. Note how much clearer everything becomes.

Rewritten Good Notes

Early European Contact with Africa   History 200
                                                           10/22/75

   I. What Drew Europeans to Africa?
     A. Gold
        There were medieval legends that there was a lot of gold in West Africa. Access to the gold was controlled by non-Christian powers (Muslims— believers in Islamic religion). Tales of gold lured the Portuguese (led by Prince Henry) to explore the coast of West Africa in the late 15th century.

By the 16th century, the Portuguese had built
several trading posts and forts along the West African
coast and were bringing back gold, ivory, and pepper.

By the 17th century, English, Dutch, French, and
Spanish ships challenged the Portuguese trading
monopoly and set up their own trading posts.
This was the beginning of rivalry between European
countries over the wealth of Africa.

B. Desire to weaken the power of the Islamic Empire
(Muslims), and expand trade with Asia

Conflict between Christianity and Islam was an
old religious conflict (the Crusades as an example
in 11th and 12th centuries). The Muslims controlled
North Africa and the Mediterranean. They also
controlled the spice trade fom Asia. Spices were
important in Europe because they were the only
known way to preserve meat.

The Catholic states of Portugal and Spain wanted
to fight with the Muslims. They wanted
to drive them out of Spain and challenge the large
Muslim empire in Africa, the Middle East, and Asia.
They hoped to convert them to Christianity.
The Muslims were strong in North Africa, but if
European powers could discover a way around
Africa into the Indian Ocean they could outflank
the Muslims and obtain direct access to the trade
with India and Asia.

C. Slaves

Portuguese trading posts in Africa had sent a small
number of slaves to Europe starting in the late
15th century. With the discovery and conquest of
America in the 16th century, a new and larger
slave trade began to European colonies in the
New World (America).

The native Indians of America died off (they were
killed in war and by European diseases). There
was a shortage of labor. In the 17th and 18th
centuries the mines of Latin America needed workers.
Large sugar plantations were set up in the Caribbean

and Brazil and cotton plantations in the southern United States. *The need for laborers to do the hard agricultural work led to the importing of millions of slaves from Africa.* Somewhere between 15 and 40 million Africans were sent to America as slaves between 1502 and the mid-19th century. This slave trade made Africa valuable to the European powers.

II. The Colonization of Africa
  A. Immigration
    Because of the unsatisfactory climate and tropical diseases, there was no major European immigration to Africa. The only significant white colony was in South Africa by the Boers (Dutch) and later the English. There were smaller European settlements in Rhodesia (English) and Algeria (French).
  B. Dividing up the continent
    1. Exploration

If you reread the poor notes now you can easily see how little of the lecture material is recorded in them and how confusing and even erroneous a picture you get from them. What is there about the poor notes that makes them inferior?

First, they are not organized. They do not even record the title of the lecture, the course number, or the date. If these notes get out of order, they will be useless. In fact, they are almost useless anyway. They are nothing more than a series of sentences about gold, trade, spices, Portugal, and slaves. The sentences are not in any particular order, and they do not say anything important. Even the factual information does not cover the major points of the lecture. Instead, it is peripheral information about sea monsters, China, Jerusalem, Bartholemew Diaz, and Columbus, most of which the good note-taker wisely omitted. By paying too much attention to trivial points, moreover, the poor note-taker missed or did not have time to record the principal theme of the lecture—the relationship between European-Asian trade and the religious struggle between Islam and Christianity. The poor note-taker also missed another major point—the connection between the enslavement of Africans and the need for plantation labor in the New World. Without these two points, this student cannot write a good exam on this subject.

The good notes, on the other hand, follow the organization of the lecture and touch upon the major points made in class. The notes make sense and can serve as the basis for reviewing the content of the lecture when studying for exams.

These notes are not crowded, but well spaced so that material and emphasis can be added later if necessary. They also have a wide margin for extra comments and the marking of important passages. (Note the emphasis on B.4 and C.5.) The instructor had emphasized these points in class, and by making special note of them, the good student will be sure to master them.

The rewritten version, which eliminates certain unimportant or repetitious phrases and smoothes the language into connected sentences, is even better as a study guide. The greatest value of rewriting, however, is that by recreating the lecture material in essay form, it becomes part of the note-taker's own thinking. The mental effort that goes into revising lecture notes serves to impress the material and its meaning upon the mind. This makes it much easier to review the material at exam time.

Class Participation

Many instructors encourage class participation, and some base a portion of the grade on it. Here are a few pointers for improving your ability to participate in class discussions.

1. Be familiar with the subject under discussion.
2. If a point is made that disagrees with your understanding, or if something in the lecture or discussion is confusing, formulate a clear question or statement in your mind.
3. If you don't get a chance to be recognized in class, bring up your question with the teacher when the session is over.
4. Teachers are not impressed with students who like to hear themselves talk or who ask thoughtless questions, but if you are interested in the subject and have

thought about what you want to say, never hesitate to speak up.

Giving a Formal Class Talk

If a course involves an oral presentation in class you must learn something about this type of assignment. Eloquence and effectiveness in public speaking cannot be mastered in a week or two, but you can make a start by taking such an assignment seriously and adequately preparing yourself for it. Reading from a prepared text is often the safest procedure, but this can lead to a dull presentation. If you speak from notes, you will have to be fully familiar with your subject and pay more attention to getting your points across. Nevertheless, this kind of presentation will probably be livelier and more enjoyable for the class. You should prepare your talk outline as you would that of a short paper (see pages 28–30). Be sure that you cover all the important points and that you present them in a logical manner. A dry run before a relative, friend, or roommate is recommended. Be sure that you exhibit a knowledge of your subject because this is most likely to determine your grade. Effective public speaking is one of the most important tools of success in many fields of work, and giving a talk in class is a good opportunity to develop your skills in this area.

chapter 3

How to Write a Book Review or Short Paper, and How to Take an Exam

Book Reviews

A book review is an essay whose purpose is to comment on a particular work or a series of works bearing upon a single subject. The most important point to remember about a book review is that it is a *commentary*, not merely a summary. Unless your instructor specifically requests that you survey the contents, a book review should spend little time outlining the material covered by the author. The bulk of your report should be an evaluation of the way the author handled the subject, and a commentary on the book's contribution to your understanding of the issues discussed. Your review should discuss the author's theme and point of view, as well as your reaction to them; evaluate the author's methodology (rules for organizing evidence); discuss the author's values and biases; and draw conclusions as to how well the author's point comes across.

It may be necessary to refer to specific portions of the book to illustrate your statements and conclusions, but it is generally not advisable to quote from it. If you know something of the author's life or other works, it is appropriate for you to make these a part of your critical evaluation. When you are reviewing several works on a common subject it is also appropriate to devote a portion of your paper to a comparison of their use of evidence, their success in supporting their themes, and their respective conclusions.

The form of a book review is similar to that of any essay. You should begin by making a list of points you wish to make. If more than two or three works are involved, do not discuss each one separately. Choose aspects of the subject that are general enough to cover all of them, and then compare the books from those particular perspectives. There is no need to give an accounting of the contents of each book.

Once your list of central points has been compiled, you should take each one as the focus of a different section of your review. (Don't try to make more points than can be accomplished in a brief book review. It is better to make a few points well than many points poorly.) Each section of your review should explain the point, support it with your own arguments and with brief examples from the book(s) under review, and then draw conclusions as to the meaning and importance of the point.

Because a book review is generally brief, come to the point directly and confine yourself to a small number of supporting examples. It should be clear to the instructor not only that you have read the book(s), but also that you have thought about what you have read and have used your own experience and critical faculties in formulating your comments.

Short Papers

A short paper (about five to ten pages) is not truly a research project. It is more of a report or essay on a particular topic based on the reading of a half dozen or so sources. A take-home essay exam is even shorter, but is organized in essentially the same way. Many of the aspects of short papers, and take-home essay exams, however, are themselves similar to the preparation of a longer research paper. (For the preparation of a research paper see Chapters 4 and 5.)

A short paper should combine a brief review of the works read in preparation for the paper with a longer development of a particular theme. The theme is the central focus of the paper, and all your references, arguments, and conclusions should be related to it. (For the development of a theme see page 65.)

Before writing your paper, you should first go through the books you have read on the subject and list the most important factual or interpretive points that you wish to use in support of your theme. You can then arrange these points in some logical progression and write a paragraph or two explaining each point and showing its connection to and support of your general theme. These paragraphs (approximately three to six pages) are the core of your text. This core should be preceded by a one- or two-page introduction, the purpose of which is to explain your theme to the reader. The core should be followed by a one- or two-page conclusion, the purpose of which is to draw together and summarize the arguments that support your theme and explain the importance of the theme and its relationship to other important issues. (For more on organizing a paper see pages 66–70.)

When the rough draft is finished, revise any section that is poorly written, that fails to support your theme, or that wanders into other subjects. Check for spelling and grammar. Read it aloud, and, keeping your reader in mind, make sure your theme comes across clearly and forcefully.

The form of a short paper can vary greatly, and you should be guided by your instructor's suggestions. If footnotes are required, one or two per page usually are sufficient, unless you are advised otherwise. In a short paper, footnote only direct quotations and especially controversial statements. (For rules regarding footnotes see pages 70–75.) In general, a short paper should not contain lengthy quotations. (For rules regarding quotations see pages 75–76.) Regardless of its size, however, a short paper should contain a bibliography. (For rules concerning bibliographies see pages 76–78.)A short paper or take-home essay should be carefully and neatly written. If possible, it should be typed double-spaced, with adequate margins on all sides. (For typing form see page 70.)

A common assignment for a short paper is the "thematic essay." Although you may be given a choice (as with a longer research paper), the topic of a thematic essay is usually assigned. The topic is an important historical issue such as the effects of the French Revolution or the causes of the American Civil War. Such issues commonly take the form of such questions as "Was American entry into World War I necessary?" and "Was the New Deal revolutionary or conservative?" The books or readings that form the basis of your research for this paper also are usually assigned. These works contain several selections—written from different points of view or using different historical evidence or methods—all of which deal with the central issue or question. When preparing a thematic essay, it is important to have the central historical issue clear in your mind and to be able to describe the major arguments and evidence of each selection in regard to that issue. (See page 12 on how to carry out an assignment involving the use of such books.)

Essay Exams

Preparing for an essay exam involves mastering the relevant course material. You will need to employ all your skills in reading course assignments and in studying your class notes. To do well in such an exam you will have to demonstrate your grasp of the subject.

Taking an essay exam can be quite a problem. You don't study, you don't study enough, you don't study the correct material, you forget what you studied, you panic in class, you don't have enough time to finish, your stomach is upset, you forget to answer a question. There is no easy way of dealing with all this, but here are a few pointers to follow until you gain the experience necessary to overcome these problems.

1. When you are given the exam don't panic. Read the entire exam slowly. Gauge the amount of time you will need to answer each question. Then choose the question you know most about to answer first.

2. Don't write the first thing that comes to your mind. Read the question slowly and be sure you understand it.
3. Determine how you will answer the question and the central points you wish to make.
4. Write these central points or even a full outline in the margin of the exam booklet, and, as you compose each sentence of your answer, make sure that it relates to one of these points.
5. Your answer must follow the question. Be as specific or general, as concrete or reflective, as the question suggests. Never allow your answer to wander away from the focus of the question.
6. Don't repeat yourself. Each sentence should add new material or advance a line of argument.
7. Where necessary, refer to the facts that support the points you are making. You must also give evidence that you have thought about the question in broad terms. The mere relation of a series of facts will rarely earn you a high grade.
8. Toward the end of your answer, you may wish to include your own opinion. This is fine, even desirable, but be sure that your answer as a whole supports this opinion.
9. Always reread and correct an answer after it is finished. The pressure of an exam can often cause you to write sentences that are not clear.
10. Write legibly, or your grader will be in no mood to give you the benefit of any doubts.
11. Don't write cute or plaintive notes on the exam. They seldom raise a grade and may prejudice the grader against you.

A well-written essay answer is a combination of (1) adequate knowledge of the subject, (2) clear thinking about the points to be covered, (3) well-structured sentences, and (4) complete understanding of the question. Following are two answers to a sample essay question on modern Chinese history. The first answer is very well written and deals success-

fully with the four requirements listed. The second answer is
very poor and meets none of these requirements.

Question: Discuss the origins of the Chinese Civil War of
1945–1949. How did the differing political programs
of the two contenders affect the outcome of that
conflict?

Good Answer

The origins of the 1945–1949 Civil War can be
traced back to the rise of Chinese nationalism in the
late nineteenth century. Out of the confusion of
the Warlord period that followed the overthrow
of the Manchu dynasty in 1911, two powerful nationalist movements arose—one reformist and the
other revolutionary. The reformist movement was
the Kuomintang (KMT), founded by Sun Yat-sen.
It was based on a mixture of republican, Christian,
and moderate socialist ideals and inspired by op-
position to foreign domination. The revolutionary
movement was that of the Chinese Communist
Party (CCP), founded in 1921, whose goal was a
communist society but whose immediate program
was to organize the working class to protect its interests and to work for the removal of foreign "im-
perialist" control.

Although these two movements shared certain
immediate goals (suppression of the Warlords, and
resistance to foreign influence), they eventually fell
out over such questions as land reform, relations
with the USSR, the role of the working class, and
the internal structure of the KMT. (The CCP oper-
ated within the framework of the more powerful
KMT during the 1920s.)

By the 1930s, when Chiang Kai-shek succeeded
Sun, the CCP was forced out of the KMT. By that
time the CCP had turned to a program of peasant
revolution inspired by Mao Tse-tung. A four-year
military struggle (1930–1934) between the two
movements for control of the peasantry of Kiangsi

Province ended in the defeat but not destruction of the CCP.

The Japanese invasion of Manchuria (1931) and Central China (1936–1938) helped salvage the fortunes of the CCP. By carrying out an active guerrilla resistance against the Japanese, in contrast to the more passive role of the KMT (which was saving its army for a future battle with the Communists), the CCP gained the leading position in the nationalist cause.

In the post–World War II period, the CCP's land reform program won strong peasant support, whereas the landlord-backed KMT was faced with runaway corruption and inflation, which eroded its middle-class following. The military struggle between 1945 and 1949 led to the defeat of the demoralized KMT army and the coming to power of the CCP.

Poor Answer

The Kuomintang had a stronger army than the Communists, but the Communists won the civil war and took over the country. Their political program, communism, was liked by the peasants because they didn't own any land and paid high taxes.

China was based on the Confucian system, which was very rigid and led to the Manchu dynasty being overthrown. The Chinese didn't like being dominated by foreigners, and Sun Yat-sen founded the Kuomintang to unite China. He believed in the Three Peoples Principles. At first he cooperated with the Chinese Communists, but later Chiang Kai-shek tried to destroy communism because he was against it. Communism was not in favor of the wealthy people.

The Communists wanted a revolution of the peasants and gave them land. They also killed the landlords. Chiang Kai-shek worried more about the Communists than about the Japanese invasion. The Japanese looked to conquer China and make it a part of their empire. Chiang Kai-shek wanted to fight the Communists first.

After World War II the Chinese Communists attacked Manchuria and took over a lot of weapons. They fought the KMT army. The KMT army lost the battles, and Chiang Kai-shek was chased to Taiwan, where he made a new government. The Communists set up their own country, and their capital was Peking. That way the Communists won the Chinese Civil War.

Let's see the differences between the poor and the well-written essay in regard to each of the four requirements for a well-written answer.

1. *Adequate knowledge of the subject.* The poor answer fails to indicate adequate knowledge in several ways. It is too brief, omitting many important facts. It describes the political programs of the two contending parties in the most vague terms. It refers to the CCP only as the Chinese Communists, leaving the impression that they were a loose grouping of like-minded individuals rather than a strong, well-disciplined political organization. It does not even mention the name of the most famous leader of the CCP—Mao Tse-tung. Chiang Kai-shek, the leader of the KMT, is mentioned, but there is no mention of his political program or beliefs, other than that he was opposed to communism. Another serious defect is the lack of chronology. The answer jumps back and forth between earlier and later periods, and no dates are given for major events.

The well-written answer illustrates a good knowledge of the subject matter. The origins, philosophies, leaders, and relationship of the two contending parties are clearly described. This answer brings in related issues such as nationalism, Warlords, guerrilla warfare against Japan, corruption, and inflation, thus indicating a broader knowledge of the historical context in which the Chinese Civil War developed. The chronology is very clear, with events proceeding in proper time sequence and with all major events identified by date.

2. *Clear thinking about the points to be covered.* The poor answer is not organized. Note that the paragraphs do not make

separate points and that each succeeding paragraph does not further develop the theme of the essay. Paragraph one is a conclusion rather than an introduction. The second paragraph goes back to the founding of the KMT, but instead of discussing the origins of the hostility between it and the CCP, it merely states that hostility came into existence. The third paragraph begins by introducing the CCP (though not by name). However, it does not expand on the CCP's programs and points of conflict with the KMT, but instead abruptly changes the focus of events and the time frame by introducing the Japanese invasion of China, which the last sentence of the paragraph only vaguely relates to the question. The last paragraph, instead of drawing conclusions about the causes of the Communist victory in the Civil War, merely states that it occurred.

The well-written answer, on the other hand, uses each paragraph to make a separate important point, and each succeeding paragraph further develops the theme of the essay. Paragraph one sets out the political programs of the two groups and the historical context in which the movements originated. The second paragraph explains the beginning of the conflict in the 1920s. Paragraph three discusses that conflict in relation to the Chinese peasantry during the early 1930s. The fourth paragraph discusses the development of the conflict in relation to the Japanese invasion of the late 1930s. The final paragraph summarizes the effects of the conflicts and of postwar developments on the outcome of the Civil War.

3. *Well-structured sentences.* Many sentences in the poor answer are badly constructed either because they are awkward or because what they say adds nothing to the answer. Some of the awkward phrases are "the Communists won the Civil War and *took over* the country"; "communism was *liked by* the peasants"; "China was *based on* the Confucian system"; "communism was not *in favor of the* wealthy people"; "the Japanese *looked to* conquer China"; "the Communists *set up their own country.*" These phrases cause the sentences to be unclear, and they keep the student from getting his or her point across. The other major defect in sentence structure is repetitious or irrelevant sentences and phrases. These are "Chiang Kai-shek tried to destroy communism *because he was against*

it"; "they *fought the KMT army*"; "that way *the Communists won the Chinese Civil War.*" The sentences of the well-written answer, on the other hand, are clear, and each adds new material to the essay.

4. *Complete understanding of the question.* The poor answer does not deal with the central issue of the question—the political programs of the KMT and the CCP. It notes that the KMT was founded on the Three Peoples Principles, but it does not explain what these were. Of the CCP, it says that there was a belief in communism (which is obvious) and peasant revolution (which is vague). These are the only references to political programs in the entire answer! It is obvious that the writer of this answer failed to understand that the central focus of the question was on political philosophy.

The well-written answer is directed to the central issue of political programs and begins on that very point. The remainder of the answer makes clear the relationship of political programs to the origins and course of the Chinese Civil War as called for in the first sentence of the question.

Objective Exams

Objective exams call for short factual answers. The questions may be multiple-choice, true-false, or definitions and identifications. If a simple choice is called for, think carefully about the alternatives before choosing. Read the question very carefully and don't jump to conclusions. If definitions or identifications are called for, answer briefly and directly. If you know only part of an answer, put that down, but don't add unrelated material just to make your answer look more impressive. You will be wasting your time. Moreover, don't try to change the question into one that you *can* answer. You won't get credit for an answer to a question that was not asked.

Take-home Exams

A take-home exam is usually a series of short essays. The construction of your answers should generally follow the procedure for writing a short paper. (See pages 28–30.) There are, however, a few specific guides to this type of assignment.

Prepare your answer by outlining those portions of the textbook or collateral readings that deal with the exam question. Then list the most important points covered in these sources—generally two to six for each question. Compose your answer by discussing each of these points in some logical order. As with all essays, it is best to have a central theme.

A problem that sometimes arises with take-home exams is plagiarism. In such an exam it is usually permissible to paraphrase the sources used in preparing your answer. Be sure, however, that you write in your own words. If you use sentences from a book in your answer you are cheating, whether you mean to or not. Copying from a text or history work is unlikely to get you anywhere. Your instructor knows that experienced historians write quite differently from students, and passages taken from such a source will jump out of the page as your paper is being read. Most instructors penalize students severely for plagiarizing. (See section on plagiarism, page 58.)

chapter 4

How to Research a History Topic

In basic history courses you may be called upon to do historical research. If you take advanced courses you certainly will be called upon to do research papers, in which case the present chapter will be helpful later. Whether you are preparing a short essay or book review or a long class presentation or term paper, you will need to know how to gather all the necessary materials and how to organize and analyze your information. This chapter will survey sources of historical information and will explain how to use these sources most profitably. The chapter also includes sections on how to record information and how to organize your notes.

Selecting a Topic

If you are given a choice of research topics, choose carefully. Doing research on a subject that does not interest you can be very boring. Try to select a topic about which you are genuinely curious. No matter what subject, person, or event you are interested in, it has a history. Every subject can be studied backward in time because every event was caused by events that preceded it. A history research project can be made out of almost anything. Perhaps in the neighborhood where you grew up there was a very old building and you had always wondered about when it was built and what it was used for. Finding out what the neighborhood was like when that building was new can be an exciting search.

An ideal topic is not only one about which you are curious, but one about which you already know something. Perhaps you read a book about Socrates and want to know more about why he was condemned to death; or perhaps you saw a movie about the depression and want to know what it was like to live through it. Instructors are eager to help students who show a real interest in a topic. Your instructor can assist you in selecting a subject related to your interests that also suits the particular course you are taking.

Formulating Your Topic

Once you have chosen a general topic (the Spanish conquest of the Aztec Empire, or the Reconstruction government of South Carolina) you should decide which specific aspect is most interesting to you, historically relevant, and most suitable to your limits of time and sources. You will not have time to properly develop a broad topic, and your sketchy treatment would not earn a satisfactory grade.

To pare down your topic to workable size ask yourself what it is that you are most interested in finding out about. If your subject is the Indians of the plains, maybe you are most curious about the practice of magic by the Blackfoot Tribe or how the Cheyenne got the swift Arabian horses they rode. Be careful that the questions you ask are not too broad ("Why did the Roman Empire Collapse?"), too narrow ("Who was the first person to sign the Declaration of Independence?"), or too unimportant ("Why are Ping Pong tables green?"). One factor determining the scope of your subject is the amount of information the library contains. When you get to the library, however, you will have a new concern: How do you find the books related to your subject? [1]

Finding Information
The best way to uncover the sources in your library is to approach the task with certain *key words* in mind. These are the words you will use when checking the card catalog. Key words, in most cases, will be the nouns that appear in the tentative formulation of your topic. For example, if your topic is the partition of India, your key word is *India*. If it is the use of the submarine in World War I, you have two key words—*submarine* and *World War I*. (Your first lesson in library language may come when you find out that some catalogs list World War I under "Great War," or "First World War.") If you have any doubts, consult the librarian to find out whether your key words are the best ones to use. This is especially advisable if your key words are very general (for example, "*conservative* thought under *Louis Napoleon*" or "*social legislation* in the early *British Empire*").

The Library Card Catalog
The main card catalog is a central file of every book in the library. Most libraries also include nonbook holdings in their main catalog. There may also be a separate catalog for periodicals and another for reference books. (If your library is very large, it is best to obtain a guide from the librarian.) Not all catalogs are organized in exactly the same way, but most set up their book card files according to author, subject, and title.

Card Catalog Information on People
If your topic is mainly concerned with a particular person (the early career of Mohandas Gandhi) you will find books by or about that person under his or her last name. These cards are known as *author cards*.

Before you start out be sure that all of your key words,

---

[1] If your school conducts a library tour for new students, be sure to take it.

especially if they are of foreign origin, are spelled correctly. If you are looking under "Gandy" or "Ghandi" instead of "Gandhi," you will have trouble.

There are two kinds of author cards, one for persons (for example, Gandhi, Mohandas; Nkruma, Kwame; Davis, Jefferson) and one for groups that publish works under their own names (for example, United States Government; Republic of France; Bethlehem Steel Corporation).

When you turn to "Gandhi, Mohandas" in the catalog, the first cards will be those for books written *by* the author. These will be arranged alphabetically according to title. If your subject is a famous person, right behind the books written by that

Library Cards: Individual Author and Group Author

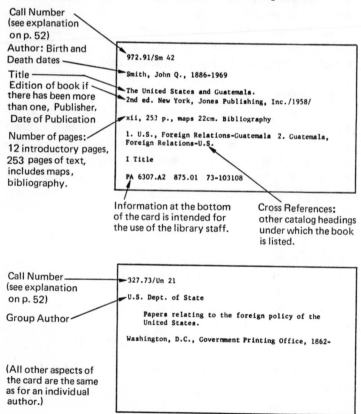

Call Number (see explanation on p. 52)

Author: Birth and Death dates

Title

Edition of book if there has been more than one, Publisher, Date of Publication

Number of pages: 12 introductory pages, 253 pages of text, includes maps, bibliography.

```
972.91/Sm 42

Smith, John Q., 1886-1969

The United States and Guatemala.
2nd ed. New York, Jones Publishing, Inc./1958/

xii, 253 p., maps 22cm. Bibliography

1. U.S., Foreign Relations-Guatemala  2. Guatemala,
Foreign Relations-U.S.

I Title

PA 6307.A2   875.01   73-103108
```

Information at the bottom of the card is intended for the use of the library staff.

Cross References: other catalog headings under which the book is listed.

Call Number (see explanation on p. 52)

Group Author

```
327.73/Un 21

U.S. Dept. of State

       Papers relating to the foreign policy of the
       United States.

Washington, D.C., Government Printing Office, 1862-
```

(All other aspects of the card are the same as for an individual author.)

person will be books written *about* him or her. These books will be listed alphabetically according to the author's last name.

Now you must determine which books by or about the person deal most directly and satisfactorily with your topic. The volumes written about Gandhi are very numerous and deal with much more than his early life. For example, a book entitled *The Assassination of Gandhi* is not likely to deal with his early years in much detail, if at all. One entitled *Gandhi's Role in the Ahmedabad Strike of 1917* will probably have too much detail on this one issue. However, because the strike was an important event in his early career, you may want to look at it. A book called *Gandhi's Influence on the Indian National Congress Party* will be a political study, and if your interest is in Gandhi's religious beliefs, it is not the best book to use. As you check through all the books on your topic, you will have to make judgments, based on the titles, as to which are most likely to contain the particular information you need. If a book title gives no clue to what aspects of your topic it concerns (for example, *My Life and Works,* or *The Career of Benjamin Disraeli*), then it is best to look at the book.

Another clue to the appropriateness of a particular book is the date of publication. For example, a book by Franklin Roosevelt, published in 1936, cannot answer questions relating to his conduct of World War II. This system is not foolproof, however, because the date of publication can be misleading. A book of poems by Mao Tse-tung might have been published in 1967, but the poems it contains may have been written many years earlier. Likewise, a book on the textile industry may appear to have up-to-date information because it was published in 1972. Nevertheless this may be the date of the third or fourth edition of a work written in 1942, which, if it hasn't been revised, can tell you nothing about postwar developments.

Your ability to squeeze the last drop of information out of the title and date of publication on the catalog card will be enhanced if you know something about your topic to begin with. If you know, for example, that Gandhi spent part of his early life in the Union of South Africa, then you know that a book entitled *Gandhi's Fight for Racial Justice in South Africa* will deal with his early career. Again, if you want to

write about the philosophy of Ralph Waldo Emerson, a book
entitled *Emerson and Transcendentalism* will leave you cold
unless you know that Transcendentalism is the name given to
a particular philosophical school. The point is to be able to
use the meager information on the catalog card to help you
choose from among the numerous listings. If you remain in
doubt about any particular book, look at the work itself.

Card Catalog Information on Places

If your key word is the name of a place, look under the
geographical nàme in the catalog. This may sound simple,
but be careful that you are using the most appropriate geographical term. Check a dictionary or atlas first to make sure
that you are spelling the term correctly. The modernization of
place names can be a problem. (For example, Russia becomes
the Union of Soviet Socialist Republics, Palestine becomes Israel, Persia becomes Iran, Peiping becomes Peking, St. Peters-
burg becomes Leningrad, Gold Coast becomes Ghana, Ciudad
Trujillo becomes Santo Domingo.) The card catalog usually
will use the most recent name, but if your topic deals with a
period when a particular place was known by another name,
you need to know that name and to look under that heading
as well. Another difficulty with place names is that some areas
become absorbed into neighboring territory and take on the
name of the larger unit. (Serbia is part of Yugoslavia, Ukraine
part of the USSR, Wales part of the United Kingdom, Zanzi-
bar part of Tanzania.) When this happens, it is best to look
under both names. Some areas have split apart, with the new
units taking on new names. (Bangladesh separated from Pakistan, West Virginia from Virginia, Republic of Ireland from
the United Kingdom, Singapore from Malaysia, Venezuela
from Gran Colombia.)

Regional names also create a problem. If your topic concerns an important region like Provence (part of France),
the Great Basin (part of the United States), the Atacama
desert (part of Chile), or Honshu (part of Japan), you will
have to check under both names. This is true as well for important political subdivisions such as Umbria (part of Italy),
Alberta (part of Canada), Jalisco (part of Mexico), Kiangsi
(part of the People's Republic of China), Queensland (part of

Australia). Knowing the correct and complete name of an area is very important. Finally, be careful with such geographical adjectives as "upper," "western," "southeast," "lesser." Some are parts of proper names; others are not. "North Dakota" is a proper name and will be found under "N," whereas "northern California" will be under "C."

Card Catalog Information on General Subjects

If your key words are general subjects, then your search through the catalog will be a more difficult task. It is tricky—like looking something up in the Yellow Pages, where, for example, car parts are under "automotive accessories" and toasters are under "electric appliances." If you can't find a subject heading in the catalog to match your key word, first check your spelling, then think of a larger subject of which your key word is a part. For example, if you can't find surgery under "S," it may be listed as a subheading under "Medicine." You might find railroads listed under "Transportation" and capital punishment under "Law." If your catalog is well constructed you will be aided by "see" or "see also" cards. If under "Wilderness Campaign" you find a card that says "see Civil War," that means your subject is listed as part of that larger topic. If you find cards listing works on your key word, you may also find one that says "see also" and gives another subject. For example, if your key word is tariff, together with the books on that subject may be a card that says "see also Trade." This means that other books related to your topic are listed under another heading. Unless you are sure that the other heading is outside the scope of your topic, see what is listed there. Many of the books may be the same, but some will be ones that were not listed under the original heading.

General Topics—Subheadings. Extremely large topics ("United States," "Economics," "Plato," "Art," "Education") are broken down in the catalog by the use of subheadings. For example, the cards on "Argentina" will be broken down into subheadings like "Argentina—Travel and Description," "Argentina—Politics," "Argentina—Relations with Brazil." Some of the subheadings will be broken down even further; for example, "Argentina—History to 1800, History 1800–1900, His-

tory 1900–present." If your topic is the politics of Juan D.
Peron, you should check "Argentina—History 1900–present"
(because Peron was in power after 1940), and you should
also check "Argentina—Politics." Because Peron is a well-
known personality, you should also check for a main heading,
"Peron, Juan D."

General topics are filed in the main catalog by *subject
cards.* These cards are filed alphabetically according to subject
heading. Within subject headings they are filed according to
author's last name. The subject and subheadings will be at
the top of the card. The remainder of the card will be the same
as for the author cards.

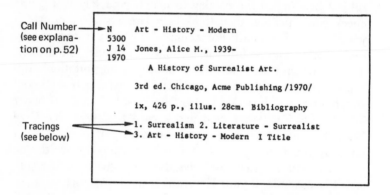

Call Number (see explanation on p. 52)

N
5300
J 14   Jones, Alice M., 1939–
1970
          Art - History - Modern

             A History of Surrealist Art.

             3rd ed. Chicago, Acme Publishing /1970/

             ix, 426 p., illus. 28cm. Bibliography

Tracings (see below)

          1. Surrealism 2. Literature - Surrealist
          3. Art - History - Modern I Title

If you are lucky, the catalog card may contain a description
of the contents of the book. If it does, as is the case with many
older catalog systems, then be sure to note the book's contents
because this is the best way to determine its relevance to your
topic. If the catalog card is of the new type originated by the
Library of Congress, it will not have any information regarding contents, but toward the bottom of the card it will have
"tracings," that is, other catalog headings under which the
particular book is listed. Though this information is more useful to librarians than to researchers, it is a clue to other headings and subheadings that might contain books on your topic.
Whenever you find a book that bears on your topic, write down
the tracings; if they seem like good leads, be sure to check
them. Some tracings will be further removed from your topic.

For example, if your topic is the atomic bombing of Hiroshima and you find a book under the catalog heading of "Atomic Energy—Military Use—World War II" that lists tracings to "Japan—World War II," this is part of your topic and should be looked into. However, if the tracing lists "Physics—Atomic Theory," this is removed from your topic and need not be pursued. The purpose of following tracings is to check every possible subject heading that might have more books on your topic. But don't get too broad in your search, or it will never end. (See section on budgeting research time, page 63.)

The Periodicals Catalog

Your library probably will have a separate catalog for periodicals or serials such as magazines, journals, and newspapers. This catalog has no subject or author headings and can be used only when you know the name of the periodical you want. The cards are filed alphabetically either by the name of the periodical or by the name of the organization that publishes it (for example, "American Academy of Political and Social Sciences—*Annals*," "American Political Science Association—*American Political Science Review*"). For a list of periodicals most useful in historical research see Appendix A, section 5.

Because this catalog tells you only which periodicals the library has and where they are located, you have to look elsewhere to find the articles that deal with your topic. Books that list periodical articles according to subject are known as periodical "guides" or "indexes." The reference section of your library should have several of them.

Different periodical indexes deal with different kinds of periodicals. Some, like the *Reader's Guide to Periodical Literature*, index popular magazines such as *Newsweek, Esquire,* and *Reader's Digest*. Others, such as the *Social Science and Humanities Index*, deal with journals written for an academic audience. (For a list of periodical indexes especially useful in historical research see Appendix A, section 4.)

Periodical indexes have special forms of organization and use special abbreviations in listing articles. At the beginning of the index is an explanation of the subject organization and the abbreviations used. Be sure to read these pages before you begin to look for articles on your subject. These pages will tell you if the subject organization of the index is different from the one used by your library card catalog. If it is very different, you will have to master it in order to find out all the subject headings in the index that relate to your key words. Among other things, the index will explain the meanings of the abbreviations of the names of the periodicals (for example, C.H. for *Current History,* H.A.H.R. for *Hispanic American Historical Review*).

When you find an article in which you are interested, be sure to copy down in full the name of the author, the name of the periodical, the title of the article, the date, the volume number, and the page numbers. You will need all of this when you return to the catalog to see if your library has the periodical you want. Moreover, the library keeps all the volumes of a particular periodical together, organized by volume and date. Unless you know the exact volume number and date of the article you want, you won't be able to find it.

A special problem that you may encounter is that smaller libraries don't receive many of the periodicals listed in the indexes. If you come up with what you feel may be a very useful article but it is in a periodical that your library does not have, ask the librarian if it is available at a larger library nearby. There are many ways of tracking down materials, but always keep in mind the time you have to prepare your work. Don't spend too much time looking for a particular source; it might be better to look deeper into your own library's resources for other materials.

Newspaper Articles

Some libraries catalog their newspaper collections in their book catalog; others put them in the periodicals catalog or in both. To find newspaper articles on your topic, however, you will have to go to *newspaper indexes.* These are published by particular newspapers and list the articles in the paper by subject and date. If your topic is the Geneva Conference of 1954, then you might want to know what a particular newspaper was reporting on that event at the time. One of the most complete newspaper indexes, and one that most libraries possess, is the *New York Times Index.* To find out what the *Times* was saying about the Geneva Conference, take the 1954 *New York Times Index* and look up "Geneva Conference" in the subject headings. Here you will find a listing of the days in 1954 on which the *Times* carried articles or editorials on the Conference. As with the periodical indexes, you will have to learn the abbreviations so that you can determine the exact place in your library's collection of the *Times* where the articles you want can be found. Again, be sure to copy down *all* relevant information.

Using newspaper articles as source materials can be very important. They are often on-the-scene and even eyewitness accounts of the particular historical event in which you may be interested. They can also contain detailed information on a particular occurrence that broad historical sources will not have. However, newspapers have their drawbacks too. First, because they are written just as an event is taking place, newspaper articles may contain inaccurate information. Second, they can tell you only *what* happened. To understand the historical significance of the event, you will have to read historical works. For on-the-scene accounts of what took place, however, there is often no substitute for newspapers. If your library's newspaper collection goes back to the years with which your subject is concerned, especially if there is an index to this collection, then it is wise to find out what those who reported the event at the time had to say about it. If your topic is broad, however, newspaper articles may not be as helpful to you. (For a list of newspaper indexes see Appendix A, section 3.)

Nonprinted Sources

Many libraries have collections of nonprinted materials, which can be useful for historical research. As technology progresses, new ways of recording the past are developed. Some of these are microfilms and other microphotography, still and motion pictures, sound recordings and tapes, and other oral history techniques. Check with the librarian to see whether your school library or one nearby has photograph, microfilm, tape, or oral history collections.

Photographs can be important pieces of historical evidence and motion pictures even more so. Oral history collections, usually consisting of recorded interviews or reminiscences by people who have been active in public life, can add both facts and excitement to historical research. Most libraries have a microfilm department where they store miniaturized photocopies of books, magazines, newspapers, and documents that the library does not have in printed form. These nonprinted sources are often filed in the main catalog along with printed works. However, it is wise to check for these sources in the special catalog that most libraries maintain. (For guides to nonprinted sources see Appendix A, section 9.)

Reference Books

A reference book is specifically designed to give you particular information or to list works on a particular subject. Reference books form such an important part of your library that they are usually shelved in a separate place, often with their own catalog.

The reference library has books to help you find materials in dissertations, archives, atlases, other libraries, government documents, encyclopedias, microfilms, yearbooks, and other places. Many of these sources are specialized and will be of use only if you go on later to do more complex historical research. There are several kinds of reference books, however, that can be helpful in the kind of research you will be doing for introductory history courses. Most important of these are bibliographies, biographies, dictionaries, and encyclopedias.

Bibliographies are usually books that list a series of works on a particular subject. These are called subject bibliographies, and there are many of these dealing with historical works. (A list of the most useful subject bibliographies can be found in Appendix A, section 7.) These works can be used to supplement the books listed in the card catalog. For example, if your topic is Chinese nationalism in the 1940s, you may want to look at the subject bibliography entitled *An Interdisciplinary Bibliography on Nationalism 1935–1953*. In the section dealing with China you will find a long list of books related to your topic. For any books that interest you, copy down *all* the information. You can then check under the author's name in the author cards to see if your library has the book. A problem with this method is that, unlike your library's card catalog, subject bibliographies list books that may not be in your library. Some of these bibliographies are very extensive and only a large university library is likely to have most of the books listed in them. If you find a book listed that you believe to be of special importance but that is not in your library, the librarian may be able to help you obtain it from another library. However, this may take time, and you should be careful not to spend too long searching for one book.

Another type of reference work that may be useful is the biography collection. These books contain outlines of the lives of well-known people. They do not contain enough information on which to base a research paper on a particular person, nor were they meant for that purpose. But they can be useful. For example, if your topic is the New York newspapers and the Spanish-American War, you may need some information concerning William McKinley, who was president during the war. By looking him up in, say, the *Dictionary of American Biography*, you will find such information as when and where he was born, his educational and religious background, the various political offices he held, and even a short description of his role in the Spanish-American War. If a particular person is a minor part of your topic, biography collections can give you much of the information you need. However, if a person is a focus of your research, you will need to read works specifically devoted to that person's life. (For biography collections most useful to historians see Appendix A, section 2.)

You should use dictionaries and encyclopedias only to become familiar with the general outline of a topic. They cannot form the basis of a research paper because they only skim the surface of a subject. If your topic is the building of the Trans-Canadian railroad, you may want to get a quick introduction to the topic by looking it up in an encyclopedia. You may also want to get some general information on the geography of the region through which the railroad was built. For this you could look under "Canada" or "British Columbia" (or some other Canadian province) in an atlas or a specialized geographical dictionary. This general overview will help you determine which headings of the card catalog will be most promising. General knowledge of your topic will also aid in selecting book titles that are closest to your subject. (See list of dictionaries and encyclopedias in Appendix A, section 1.)

Locating Materials and Using Call Numbers

When you come across a book or periodical in the catalog that you think might contain relevant source material, be sure to copy down all the relevant information. (It may not seem important at the time, but if you eventually use the volume in your research, you will have to include this information in your footnotes and bibliography. If you don't get the complete data now you will only have to return to the catalog later to look it up again.) Also copy down the call numbers—the classification numbers in the upper left-hand corner of the catalog card. Without them neither you nor the librarian will be able to find the materials you want.

The call number indicates where the book is located. If your library is one where only the librarian takes the books from the shelves, then you only have to write down the call numbers of the books you want. If your library has "open stacks," that is, book shelves to which readers have access, then you will need to know something about the classification system.

There are two classification systems in general use—the Dewey Decimal system and the Library of Congress system. The Dewey call numbers begin with a *numeral;* the Library of Congress call numbers begin with a *letter.* They are both complex systems, though once you master the principles, you will have an excellent road map to your library's shelves. If the stacks are open, obtain from the librarian a pamphlet explaining the classification system. Without the pamphlet you will waste a lot of time looking for the books you want. (An explanation of these two systems can be found in Appendix B.)

If you get to the place in the shelves where you think the book should be and it is not there, you are facing one of several problems: (1) the book is in use by another reader; (2) it has been transferred to another part of the library; (3) it has been shelved incorrectly; or (4) you have an incorrect call number.

When you find the book you want, it is wise to look at the books on the surrounding shelves because they will be on related subjects. Once you find a book, however, your search is not finished. Now you need to determine its relevance to your subject.

Determining Whether a Book Will Be of Use

Once you have a book, you must determine whether it deals with your specific topic and whether its approach is appropriate for you. Book titles can be misleading. *The Election of Woodrow Wilson* may turn out to be about the inner workings of the Democratic Party. If you are preparing a paper on Wilson, this book may not be of much use to you, despite its title. Even when a book deals specifically with your topic, its handling of the subject may make it less than satisfactory. For example, a book that is written for less advanced students, even though it is on your topic, will not make a good source. Its coverage will be general and it may gloss over or omit important facts or interpretations that your research should include. A glance at the introduction should help you determine the kind of readers for which the book was written.

Another problem you may encounter is the author's viewpoint or bias. For example, a history of World War I by a French author is likely to have a different viewpoint from one written by a German author, especially if the books were written close to the time of the war. It is very important for you to understand the point of view from which a book was written. Many historical events and their interpretation are the centers of profound controversy. It is almost impossible for a historian to investigate one of these controversial areas without the involvement of certain biases. A particular attitude toward the topic is not necessarily bad, however. Historical problems are immensely complex, and without a sense of which things are important, the historian will not be able to choose from among all the facts of the situation those that can give some clear meaning to the larger questions involved. In any event, it is important for you to become familiar with the biases of the authors you read so that you will not unknowingly accept their viewpoints. If you agree with an author's bias, it is natural that you will favor his or her work in your research. But unless you understand the biases of the authors you read, and your own as well, you will not know why you agree with some authors more than others. Furthermore, you won't be able to make a logical presentation in your research paper of the varying points of view.

The first place to check for determining the usefulness and bias of a book is its table of contents. Although some chapter titles are vague, most will give you a clearer picture of the contents than the work's title. If your topic is the Caribbean policy of Theodore Roosevelt, and you have come upon a book entitled *The Era of Theodore Roosevelt,* you will be pleased to find a chapter called "Hemisphere Diplomacy." Though the entire work may be of value to you, it is this chapter that will contain the most material on your specific topic. On the other hand, if the chapter headings are all concerned with Roosevelt's domestic policies or the cultural, scientific, and intellectual trends of the early 1900s, there may be little in the book on foreign policy.

If the chapter headings are not clear enough for you to determine the book's usefulness, your next move is to look at the index. Not every book has an index, but when one does, it is an invaluable tool. The index lists in alphabetical order the pages on which different persons or subjects are discussed. The index in a book on the Progressive Party in Wisconsin will list each of the pages on which Robert M. LaFollette is mentioned. It may even break this down and tell you which pages discuss LaFollette's early career, which his campaigns for the presidency, and so on. When the scope of a book is very broad, the index is the best guide to find that portion of it that is closest to your topic. Remember, however, that unless you read more of the book than just those pages which deal with your topic, you will not know the author's biases or conclusions, and these may be of great importance. Although you may want to select only small portions of a book to use in your research, if any of your own conclusions are drawn from a particular work, you will need to know its overall contents.

If the book has no index, or if you wish to get the flavor of the work as a whole before selecting it as a source for your paper, the introduction and bibliography may be of help. Authors often explain some of their purposes and conclusions in the introduction, and a look at the bibliography (if one is included) will give clues as to what sources the author felt were important and how extensive his or her own research was.

Perhaps the best way to gain an overall impression of a work is to skim its contents by reading the introductory paragraph of each chapter and perhaps the introductory sentence to each paragraph in those parts of the book that seem most important. If you have mastered a method of rapid reading, that skill will be very useful here. Once you have chosen a book for your research, of course, there is no substitute for careful reading.

Reading Books

Reading books may sound easy but, unless you have had experience in reading serious historical studies, you may have problems. First of all, some of the vocabulary may be new to you. A book on the French Revolution will contain such words as Jacobin, Thermidore, and Girondin. A study of the atom bomb will talk about implosion and fission and such places as Tinian and Eniwetok. It is best to have a good dictionary handy. Another problem will be the academic or scholarly style of writing often found in specialized works. You will come across sentences like this:

> Despite the innumerable, and often contradictory, intellectual themes reflected in the ideological position taken by the right wing of the movement, it nevertheless managed, despite the defection of a small fascist element, to maintain the loyalty of the land-owning peasantry of the Central Highlands as well as the professional and shopowners associations of the capital, not to mention that of several union organizations which still maintained a craft orientation.

By the time you finish such a sentence, you may have forgotten how it began. To make matters worse, such tongue-twisters are often filled with words like: balkanization, corporativism, Hegelianism, Mandate of Heaven, negritude, neomercantilism, Pan-Slavism, Pax Romana, popular front, primogeniture, Reconquista, shogunate, Trotskyism, utilitarianism, White Terror, or Zoroastrianism. Unfortunately there is no shortcut to understanding such terminology. As you become familiar with your topic, you will learn the meanings of the terms used by scholars. The only way to get through the complex prose is to have a good background in English grammar and a familiarity with the subject being discussed. Therefore, among the books you have chosen for your research, you should read first the most general and then the more specialized ones.

As you become familiar with the style and terminology used in a work, your main task will be to understand the points the author is trying to establish. All good works of history do more than just lay out a series of historical events and then combine them to form an understandable story of what occurred. Good historians want to prove a point, to show that a series of historical events mean one thing rather than another. A history of the rise of Adolf Hitler won't merely tell you that the National Socialist Party, which he led, increased the number of its representatives in the German Reichstag (parliament) from 12 to 107 in the elections of 1930. It will attempt to describe the conditions that led to such an outcome and to explain the impact of the election on later events. Perhaps the author will discuss unemployment, German nationalism, the cartelization of German industry, the Treaty of Versailles, the growth of the German Communist Party, anti-Semitism, the structure of the German family, the philosophy of Nietzsche, or the insecurity of the lower middle class. The author will probably deal with some of these more extensively than others, and will attempt to show how the emphasized factors offer a better explanation of the subject than any others. Although almost all historians will agree on the number of National Socialist members of the 1930 Reichstag, each will construct the causes and effects of that fact in different ways—sometimes in *very* different ways. If you wish to understand a particular author's interpretation of an event, you must know how the author arrived at that interpretation and what significance he or she believes it to have. Only a careful reading of the entire work and close attention to the book's main arguments can give you such knowledge. Remember, history books are a selection of certain facts and interpretations constructed to explain a particular writer's understanding of a historical subject. If your own research relies heavily on a particular book, you will need to know its theme and bias.

Taking Notes

As you go through a book, you will find portions that you will want to refer to in your own research paper. You will want to note the author's general idea or perhaps even record the actual words used. If you wish to quote, be careful to copy down exactly the words in the book. Be sure that the meaning of the words you quote is clear and that you have not altered the author's point by quoting it out of context. If you wish to use a quotation, say, to show that Robert E. Lee was a good military strategist, a quotation such as "Lee was more admired by the average soldier than any other commanding officer" doesn't make that point because it refers to his popularity, not his generalship. Moreover, if the following sentence in the book is "However, his strategic decisions were not usually equal to those of Union army commanders," then you have actually altered the author's point by taking it out of its original context. Make sure you understand the author's meaning before you use a quotation.

The most important points made by an author usually cannot be summed up in easily quotable form. When you want to record general arguments and conclusions, it is best to write your own paraphrase or summary of particular points. If the author has spent several pages relating the decline in trade between Spain and Mexico to the Wars of Mexican Independence, you may want to summarize the findings by noting that the author feels that the diminishing economic tie between colony and mother country was one of the major factors leading to Mexican independence. If you wish to note the evidence itself, you may want to paraphrase the author's description of the decline in trade with several sentences of your own that include the main factors of this decline.

Whether you are quoting an author's exact words or summarizing a point, the rules of note-taking are the same. As you read it is best to have a pile of index cards beside you (4" x 6" or 5" x 8" are usually best). When you come to something you want to note, write the author's name, the book title, and the page number or numbers at the top of the card.[2] The exact

[2] If you are taking notes on a journal or newspaper article you will need to record such information as date, volume number, page and column number.

page numbers are essential because you will have to use them when you write your footnotes. Also, it is wise to place each summary or quotation on a separate card.

If you are quoting, be sure to use quotation marks and to copy the quotation word-for-word. If you are quoting something that the author has quoted, you must be sure to point this out when you use the material and to identify the original source. If a quotation is very long and if there are parts that relate to matters other than the one you are referring to, then you may omit portions of the original quote by inserting ellipses, three periods (. . .), in the quoted material.[3] For example, if the quotation reads "Feudalism, despite later idealizations of it, was maintained by an oppressive social order," you may want to leave out "despite the later idealizations of it," and quote the sentence as "Feudalism . . . was maintained by an oppressive social order." However, never omit anything if that would change the meaning of the material. If the sentence had read "Feudalism in its later stages in Moravia was maintained by an oppressive social order," the entire sentence would have to be quoted, or its meaning would be seriously altered.

Avoiding Plagiarism

The only thing worse than misquoting from your sources is plagiarizing from them. Plagiarism is easy to fall into. Because of your inexperience with your subject, it will be tempting to use the more sophisticated language of the historians you are reading. In most cases, their expertise will enable them to make their point clearly, and it is easy to get into the habit of using their words instead of your own. Don't fall into this trap. First of all, your instructor is also a historian and can tell the difference between the language of someone who has spent years researching a topic and that of the average history student. Second, and more important, is the fact that thinking is learning. If you substitute the simple task of copying for the more

---

[3] If the portion omitted is the end of a sentence, this is indicated by inserting four periods—three to indicate omission and the fourth to indicate the end of the original sentence. In this case, the closing quotation mark appears after the fourth period.

difficult but rewarding one of thinking about something and then putting it into your own words, then you are doing yourself a disservice.

To help you avoid plagiarism, here is a passage from a history work followed by two paraphrasings. Paraphrase *a* constitutes plagiarism, but *b* does not. The subject is the diplomacy of Woodrow Wilson. Here is the original text:

> Wilson took personal responsibility for the conduct of the important diplomacy of the United States chiefly because he believed that it was wise, right, and necessary for him to do so. Believing as he did that the people had temporarily vested their sovereignty in foreign affairs in him, he could not delegate responsibility in this field to any individual. His scholarly training and self-disciplined habits of work made him so much more efficient than his advisers that he must have thought that the most economical way of doing important diplomatic business was for him to do it himself. Experience in dealing with subordinates who sometimes tried to defeat his purposes also led him to conclude that it was the safest method, for he, and not his subordinates, bore the responsibility to the American people and to history for the consequences of his policies.

Paraphrase a

Wilson took personal responsibility for conducting diplomacy because he believed it was right for him to do so. Believing that the people had vested their sovereignty in foreign affairs in him, he couldn't delegate this responsibility. His scholarly training and self-discipline made him more efficient than his advisers. He thought that the most economical way of doing important business was to do it himself. Experience in dealing with subordinates who sometimes tried to defeat his purposes led him to conclude that it was the safest method because he bore responsibility to the American people for the consequences.

Paraphrase b

Wilson felt personally responsible for major diplomacy because he believed that the voters had entrusted him with such matters. He was more capable than his advisers in this area. He, and not his advisers, was responsible to the people.

Paraphrase *a* is too close to the original. Rather than recording the main points of the passage, it repeats many phrases word-for-word. Not only is it time-consuming to take such lengthy notes, but the identical and almost identical phrases, if used as your own, would constitute plagiarism. The second paraphrase records only the principal point of the passage—that Wilson decided major foreign policy issues on his own because he felt personally responsible to the people in such matters. It does not copy the phraseology of the original. In this way, you save time, avoid plagiarism, and still are able to use the central idea of the passage. Paraphrasing that reduces your readings to their essential points and utilizes your own words is not easy at first. But mastering this technique will prevent plagiarism and produce a finished paper that is truly yours.

Outlining and Organizing

When you have read all the sources on which you will base your own paper or presentation, you should have a series of index cards, each with a separate quotation, commentary, or summary of a point made, and each with the complete identification of the source from which it is taken.

In order to organize your notes, you need to make a tentative outline of your paper. If your topic is American blacks and the depression, you may decide to deal with the topic chronologically and separate your paper into sections dealing with the period before 1929, the Hoover years, the early New Deal, and the late New Deal. Or perhaps you want to cover the subject topically, setting up separate sections on black reactions to economic discrimination, the National Association for the Advancement of Colored People, the U.S. Communist Party, organized labor, and New Deal legislation. Or perhaps you will want to consider the ideas of important black leaders and writers of the day, setting up sections dealing with E. Franklin Frazier, Richard Wright, Ralph Bunche, W. E. B. Du Bois, A. Philip Randolph, Langston Hughes, and Claude McKay.

A chronological approach begins with events that predate those that are the main focus of the paper. It then moves, step by step, through stages that group together spans of time. These spans may be in years, decades, or—for a very broad topic—centuries. Each time span is later than the one preceding it, and they generally do not overlap.

Time spans do not have to be the same length. It is best to use larger time units when discussing events that occurred long before the main events covered in the paper and to use smaller units when covering the period closest to the main events. A different rule applies to the length of each *section* of the paper: Those portions dealing with periods removed from central events should be more brief than those portions close in time to such events.

A common problem with chronological organization is determining how far back in time to begin. Do you start ten or a hundred years before the time of the main events of the paper? A similar problem is determining where to stop. Do you stop with the main events themselves, or do you add sections covering later periods as well? There is no hard and fast rule, but it is wise not to cover too much ground. That is, don't start too long before or end too long after the principal events of your topic. A paper covering several hundred years is very unwieldy, and is best not handled by the chronological form of organization.

A topical form of organization is usually best for more general themes—those that deal with ideas, social systems, or other complex phenomena that involve a mixture of political, social, economic, cultural, and intellectual backgrounds. In this form of organization the task is not so much to build a historical sequence leading up to a particular event, but to weave a fabric composed of the many separate lines of historical development that form the background to the main topic. In many cases, the same topic can be organized by either method. If you have trouble choosing, or if you wish to explore other forms, your instructor should be able to help you.

To give you an idea of how a particular topic might be organized by each of the two methods, here are sample tables of contents of two papers called "The United States and the War in Vietnam."

Chronologically:

Introduction
- I. The United States and the French War in Vietnam, 1946–1954
- II. The Geneva Conference of 1954
- III. The Eisenhower Administration and the South Vietnamese Government of Ngo Dinh Diem, 1954–1960
- IV. Military Involvement under President Kennedy, 1961–1963
- V. Escalation under President Johnson, 1964–1968
- VI. Negotiation and Troop Withdrawals under President Nixon, 1969–1973
- VII. Conclusion—The United States and Vietnam Today

Topically:

Introduction
- I. United States Economic and Political Interests in Vietnam
- II. The History of Communism in Vietnam
- III. United States Foreign Policy and Vietnam
- IV. Congress and the War
- V. The Antiwar Movement in the United States
- VI. The Politics of the Republic of South Vietnam
- VII. The Vietnam War and International Relations
Conclusion

However you choose to organize your paper, you must organize your notes in the same manner. One of the best ways to do this is to read each of your note cards and mark it according to that part of the paper to which it applies. You may also want to describe briefly the contents of each card at the top. Then, when you prepare the final organization of your paper, you can arrange all your notes within each section according to the subjects to which they refer. (See section on organization, pages 66–67.)

Budgeting Research Time

If you are writing, say, a fifteen- to thirty-page paper, expect to read about a dozen sources. This is not a firm figure, however, and your teacher and the subject you choose are better guides to the proper amount of research. If you read too few sources, your work will be shallow and perhaps unsatisfactory. If you read too many, you will not complete your work in the allotted time. It is best to make a tentative bibliography early in your research and discuss its adequacy in terms of topicality, authoritativeness, and length with your instructor. Discussion with your teacher of the preliminary outline for your paper should take place about this time also.

If you have never before written a long research paper, you may be unsure as to how much time to allot to each aspect of your research and writing. Only experience will tell you the best budget of time for your particular work habits, but here are some general rules.

For a paper of fifteen to thirty pages due at the end of a fifteen-week semester, you should allow approximately 10 percent of your time (one to two weeks) for choosing a topic, preparing a tentative bibliography, and familiarizing yourself with the general contours of your topic; about 60 percent (seven to eight weeks) reading the available research materials and taking notes from them; about 10 percent (another week) thinking and talking about what you have read and organizing your notes; and about 20 percent (two to four weeks) for writing and typing the preliminary and final drafts.

If your term is much shorter than fifteen weeks, or if your assignment must be finished before the end of the semester, you will need to shorten your budget accordingly. (For a discussion of the preparation of papers of five to fifteen pages see Chapter 3.) Remember that by the end of the term exams will dominate your attention, and a paper due the final week of classes is best finished at least a week before that time so as not to conflict with studying for finals.

Historical Materials Outside the Library

If you are fortunate, your topic will be one on which special historical materials are available at a nearby special collections library, a museum, a historical society, the archives of an institution or corporation, or film and audio tape libraries of television and radio studios.

Older members of your community or your own family also can be sources of historical information. People who have been leaders in local and national affairs have personal knowledge of important historical events. Perhaps you could prepare a series of questions concerning past events in which they were participants. You can write to these individuals, or perhaps speak with them. They may also have personal papers they would permit you to see. This kind of historical research is exciting and satisfying, and it may enable you to use primary historical material that no other historian has uncovered.

Elderly people are very good sources of historical material. They can tell of their years in another country or describe the America of fifty years ago in which they grew up. They may not have made history, but they experienced it. Their recollections of how they felt and of what others did and said when, for example, the Titanic sank, when Lindburgh flew across the Atlantic, or when Babe Ruth hit a record-breaking home run are priceless pieces of the historical puzzle. Of course your family is the best and perhaps only source of its *own* history (genealogy). To research the history of your family is to re create a portion of the historical experience of our country and also to become aware of your own place within that experience. Moreover, knowing your family's history and its meaning can give you strong emotional and intellectual roots that will serve to strengthen you throughout your lifetime.

chapter 5

How to Write a Research Paper [1]

The Theme

It is impossible to write a complete history of your subject, and you should not try. A good research paper will give the basic facts and interpretations concerning a subject, but it should not become a record of everything you have read. Your aim in writing a history research paper is to use your knowledge of the subject to develop a particular *theme*—a central point, assertion, or argument for the facts and interpretations of your paper. The goal of your writing should be to introduce the theme clearly, support it effectively, and then draw meaningful conclusions about it.

[1] This chapter contains generally accepted guides to writing style. Check to see if your instructor has any specific preferences which may vary from these.

Instead of merely describing the life of someone, the course of a war, or the outcome of an election, your paper should take a stand and make assertions. For example, a paper on the siege of the Alamo should do more than tell the story of the battle. It should make some central point about the siege and argue its importance. Your instructor will not be satisfied with a paper that describes the nature of the fortifications, relates how many died, and concludes that the defenders were very brave. You must find some theme that explains the causes of the battle or that relates the event to larger issues. Perhaps you will want to discuss the morale of both forces and relate the course and outcome of the battle to the fighting ability of the Mexican army or to the cause of Texas independence. If your subject is the early career of Chiang Kai-shek, instead of merely relating the major events of his life, choose a theme such as the effect of the Bolshevik Revolution on his thinking or how his ideas on land reform influenced his relationship with the Chinese Communist Party. With your thematic focus, your facts and arguments become relevant, and your paper develops them logically and clearly.

Organization

You can now break down your subject into those elements that best illustrate your theme. From your reading you should be familiar with those aspects of it that were given prominence, or that you yourself have concluded are important. The outline of your paper should include sections that deal with these important areas in a way that relates them to your theme. For example, if your subject is the conflict between Israel and its Arab neighbors, your research may have determined that two basic elements of the subject are Zionism and Arab nationalism, and that two important events were the Balfour Declaration of 1917 and the United Nations Partition Plan of 1947. If most or all of your sources mention these as important, then you must find a place for them in your outline so that you will not fail to cover them in your paper.

When a point is not stressed by your sources but you have concluded that it is of significance to your theme, it should, of course, be included. For example, if your theme is Nasser's commitment to Arab nationalism, and after researching the Arab-Israeli dispute you conclude that Nasser's reaction to his experiences in the war of 1948 was an important factor in his later conduct, then, even if your sources treated this matter very lightly, you will want it to appear in your outline.

When constructing an outline, be sure that you have enough facts to support each separate item. You cannot deal effectively with the issue of Nasser's experience in 1948 unless your notes contain evidence to support your point of view. Although you are free to draw your own conclusions from what you have read, your paper should not emphasize unsupported views you may have. If you feel very strongly about a particular point, but don't find it supported by your research, then you must try to find some corroboration for your views. Even without support from other sources, however, you can still state your own opinions in your paper, but they should be clearly labeled as such.

In addition to pursuing your theme and covering the important points made in your reading, your outline should include an introduction and conclusion. The introduction should state the central theme and explain why you think the topic is important or interesting. The conclusion should sum up the major points, explain how they sustain your central theme, and discuss the importance of your theme for other subjects.

When constructing an outline, be sure that the sections are in a logical order. If you are treating your subject chronologically, each part of the outline must be in date order. If you are dividing your subject topically, each topic must raise a separate issue. Always keep in mind that the purpose of your outline is to develop your theme. If your subject is the role of the peasantry in the Mexican Revolution, and your theme is that the peasants' military role was crucial to the outcome of the Revolution, then the political philosophy of the liberal landowner Francisco Madero, regardless of its importance, should not be a part of your outline. Each part of the outline must pass two tests: Does it relate to the theme, and does it deal with a different aspect of the theme than the other parts of the outline? (For sample outlines see pages 60–62.)

Writing the Text

Once you have prepared your outline and separated your notes according to the parts of the outline to which they correspond, you will need to judge how long each section of the paper should be. The length and number of sections will vary according to the subject matter and the type of assignment, but here is a general guide: If your paper is to be about twenty-five pages long, it is best not to have more than six or seven sections. You will need at least three or four pages to treat adequately each of the points you want to cover. As you write each section, keep in mind the information you wish to include and the principal points you wish to develop. Form that section around the corresponding notes, making sure that you explain the relationships among the facts you present.

Your paper as a whole should contain an introduction, a central development (the body) and a conclusion. Likewise, each section should set out its particular point, move through the development of that point, and close with material that relates that point to those that follow. If your topic is German aid to the forces of General Francisco Franco in the Spanish Civil War, then the section that deals with the reasons behind German support might begin by briefly describing the circumstances surrounding Franco's appeal to Hitler in 1936. The main body of the section would explain in some detail Hitler's reasons for giving aid (for example, strategic and economic considerations, ideological and diplomatic factors) and would conclude by relating these reasons to the subject of later sections such as the actual aid given and its effect on the course of the war. Your principal concerns as you construct each section of your paper should be: Does this section follow logically from the one preceding it; does it adequately support and develop the central theme; and does it establish the necessary background for the section that follows?

As each section mirrors the overall structure of the paper by containing an introduction, development, and conclusion, so each paragraph of which the section is composed contains a similar structure. A well-constructed paragraph begins with a sentence that introduces the information to be developed and concludes with a sentence that summarizes that information. If each paragraph is developed in this way, and if sentences explaining the relationship between paragraphs are included where necessary, then the paper as a whole becomes a tightly knit series of related statements rather than a random group of facts that do not seem to move in any clear direction. The key to tight construction is for each sentence to have two components: It must be related to the one preceding it, and it must continue the development of the theme to which it is related.

Here are two groups of sentences. The first is tightly constructed; the second is not.

> In 1919, most Germans felt that the terms of the Versailles Treaty were harsh. In particular, they believed that the reparations and war-guilt clauses of the Treaty were unjust. When Hitler rose to power fourteen years later, he appealed to this sense of injustice in order to gain support for his program of denouncing the Treaty.

> In 1919, most Germans felt that the terms of the Versailles Treaty were harsh. The French hoped to weaken German war-making capacity by forcing her to pay heavy war reparations. Hitler appealed to the German people to support his program to denounce the Treaty.

Despite the fact that each sentence in the second version is true, the paragraph does not hang together because the sentences are not clearly related. The first sentence refers to German feelings about the treaty, and then the second jumps to a discussion of French attitudes and drops the reference to the Versailles Treaty, which is the common theme that ties together the sentences of the first version. The third sentence further confuses the situation by jumping back to Germany and forward in time without any proper transition. On the other hand, the first version is tightly constructed because the second sentence, rather than breaking the line of development by bringing in a new element, expands and accentuates the point made in the first. The third sentence explains the forward jump in time and relates the events of the later period (Hitler's denunciation of the Treaty) to the German people's sense of injustice established in the first two sentences.

The best way to insure that there are no logical gaps between your sentences is to construct each paragraph from the viewpoint of the average person who might read your paper. Very often, a disconnected set of sentences may seem clear to you because as you write them you unconsciously fill in the gaps with your own knowledge. Your reader most likely does not have this knowledge and has to depend entirely on the words you write. If these are not enough to make your point clearly, you must be more explicit.[2]

It is often helpful to put your paper aside for a day or two and then reread it. By doing so, you can often gain a fresh perspective and can detect weaknesses that you hadn't noticed before.

Typing Form

Choose a medium- or heavy-weight paper for your final copy. It is wise to make a copy of your work in case part or all of the original is lost. Leave at least an inch margin on all sides. (Sometimes an inch and a half on the left margin is preferable.) Double-space the text except for long quotations and footnotes. Give each page a consecutive number in the upper right-hand corner. Prepare a separate title page that includes the title (underlined) and your full name. Also include any information that may be needed to identify the work, such as the name and number of the course, the day and time of meeting or section number, the instructor's name, and the date. Check with your instructor for specific instructions.

Footnotes

What to Footnote. Footnotes give the source of the facts and opinions that appear in your paper. If you quote, paraphrase, or summarize from your research materials, you must say where the original information can be found. This is done

---

[2] The other basic component of clarity is a well-constructed sentence. No matter how well sentences are linked to one another, if the sentences themselves have faulty grammatical construction, the result will be unsatisfactory. If your sentence writing ability is weak, you should look into one of the grammar and style manuals listed in Appendix B.

so that the reader can check the accuracy of your statements, judge the bias and credibility of your sources, and carry out research of his or her own. On occasion you may also want to use footnotes to make comments that supplement or qualify statements in your text.

A question that always troubles students is which statements in a paper need to be footnoted. There are no hard and fast rules concerning the use of footnotes. A professional scholar's criteria will be different from those of a student or amateur researcher. For the student writing a fifteen- to thirty-page term paper, three types of statements should be documented: (1) direct quotations, (2) controversial facts or opinions, and (3) statements that directly support the main points made in the paper.

All direct quotations must be footnoted. Controversial facts or opinions are those that not all of your sources agree on. If you state that most slave-masters in Mississippi were kind to their slaves, and you know from your research that there are authors who strongly dispute this, then you must footnote that statement. A fact or opinion is also controversial if it is something with which the average reader would disagree. For example, you may have found that all your sources agree that Vikings visited the New World long before Columbus. However, if most people believe that Columbus was the first European to see the New World, then it is necessary to show your reader the source of your information with a footnote. Finally, statements of fact or opinion that directly support main points should be footnoted. If your subject is the Protestant Reformation, and you treat nationalism as a major factor in the break with Catholicism, then your references in the text to nationalist forces should be footnoted. On the other hand, if you treat the wealth of the Catholic Church as a very minor factor, then your references to that need not be footnoted.

The number of footnotes to use is another thorny problem. Some papers have more factual or controversial material than others and thus need more footnotes. As a rule of thumb, if your paper has quite a few pages without any footnotes, then you are probably not documenting as much as you should. On the other hand, if you are writing five or more footnotes per page, you may be overdoing it. There is no such thing as the *right* number of footnotes, but a twenty-five page paper might contain anywhere from fifteen to seventy-five footnotes, depending on the subject.

How to Write Footnotes. When you decide that a footnote is necessary, place a number at the end of the sentence that contains the information to be documented. Occasionally, you may want to footnote two different things in the same sentence. In this case, place each number right after the word or phrase you want to footnote. Some writers place the number at the end of a paragraph rather than at the end of a sentence. This is proper only if the footnote refers to the material in the paragraph as a whole. If you are footnoting specific facts or quotations, the number should appear just after the facts or quoted material. If you are footnoting a general idea or opinion, place the number at the end of the paragraph or paragraphs that discuss them. All footnote numbers should be placed a half space above the line of typing. The number should not be put in parenthesis and should be inserted after any punctuation (except a dash).

Some writers put their footnotes at the bottom of the page. This is the form used in many of the books you will use in your research. It is easier for the reader, but it creates problems for the typist, who must judge how much space to leave at the bottom of the page. An easier form, and one that is acceptable to most instructors, is to put all the footnotes at the end of the paper. If you use this method, you must number your footnotes consecutively throughout the work and write them on a separate piece of paper as you compose the rough draft.

Footnote Form. The footnote form illustrated here is a simplified one geared to beginning students.[3] If you have sources that do not fit into these rules, you can check a more advanced manual such as Kate L. Turabian, *Student Guide for Writing College Papers* (Chicago: University of Chicago Press, 1969)

---

[3] Check to see if your instructor prefers a different form.

There are two basic forms for writing footnotes, one for books and one for articles:

Books

> Crane Brinton, A Decade of Revolution 1789–1799 (New York: Harper and Brothers, 1934), pp. 18–22.

1. Author's name in full, followed by a comma.
2. Title in full, underlined.
3. Publication information (enclosed in parentheses and followed by a comma): place of publication, followed by a colon; name of publisher, followed by a comma; date of publication.
4. Page or pages cited, followed by a period.

Some book footnotes are more complex. If a book has several authors, or if it has a translator or editor, or was published in several volumes or editions, then the footnote has to include such information. For example:

> T. W. Wallbank and A. M. Taylor, Civilization Past and Present, Vol. II, rev. ed. (Chicago: Scott Foresman, 1954), pp. 12, 104–117.

Note that when there are two authors, both are listed. If there are more than three authors, the footnote includes the name of the one listed first in the book followed by "et al." (and others). If there is more than one volume to a work, the volume used as a source must be specified and inserted after the title. If the particular book used is a later edition of the work, that too is inserted after the title. Note also from the example that pages from two different parts of the same book can be covered in one footnote. If there is an editor or translator, that person's name, followed by "ed." or "trans." appears in the place reserved for the author's name:

> Eugene C. Black, ed., Posture of Europe 1815–1940 (Homewood, Ill.: Dorsey Press, 1964), p. 102.

Articles

> Dana F. Fleming, "The Role of the Senate in Treaty Making," American Political Science Review, XXVIII (August, 1934), p. 583.

1. Author's name in full, followed by a comma.
2. Title of article, followed by a comma, all in quotation marks.
3. Title of periodical (journal or magazine), underlined and followed by a comma.
4. Volume number, date in parenthesis, followed by a comma.
5. Page or pages cited, followed by a period.

If the article is an editorial or has no author, the footnote begins with the name of the article:

> "America's Interest in the Cuban Economy," Barrons, XVI (January 20, 1936), p. 9.

This form is common for popular magazines, editorials, and many newspaper articles.

For specialized sources such as unpublished materials, book reviews, microfilm, speeches, dissertations, interviews, government documents, private correspondence, and radio or television programs, see a more specialized book, such as Turabian.[4]

A final rule about footnotes regards *second references* to the same source. If you refer to a particular book or article in more than one footnote, only the first reference has to have all of the information. The second reference to the *same* book need include only the author's last name and the page number.[5] If your first footnote read

> Robert F. Kennedy, Thirteen Days (New York: W. W. Norton & Co., 1969), p. 14.

your second and later references would read simply

> Kennedy, p. 123.
> Kennedy, p. 168.

If, however, you are also referring to other books by Robert Kennedy, you will have to repeat the title so your reader knows to which book you are referring.

The second time you refer to an article, you need to repeat

---

[4] For a common list of abbreviations used in footnotes see Appendix B.

[5] Some instructors prefer second references to include a shortened title as well as the author's last name and the page number.

only the name of the author and the page.[6] Thus if your first footnote to an article read

> Julius W. Pratt, "American Business and the Spanish-American War," Hispanic American Historical Review, XIV (May, 1934), pp. 184–187.

your second and later references would read simply

> Pratt, pp. 189–191.

Again, if you are also referring to another article or book by Pratt, later references will have to include the name of the book or article.

Whenever you write a footnote, ask yourself: Is it clear to the reader exactly which source I am referring to, and does that reader have enough information to find that source if necessary?

Quotations

What to Quote. Don't quote too often, and don't make quotes too long. Many students tend to rely on other people's words more than necessary. Unless the exact words of your source are crucial to making an important point, or unless great controversy surrounds the statement, it is not necessary to use a quotation. In most cases a paraphrase or summary of the statement, properly footnoted, is sufficient. If you do quote, be sure to quote enough of the original statement to make its meaning clear, but do not make the quote any longer than necessary. Remember that a quotation must clearly be labeled as such and the speaker clearly identified.

Quotation Form. If a quotation is brief, taking up no more than two or three lines of your paper, then it should be written as a part of the text and surrounded by quotation marks. You should introduce the quotation with a clear identification of the speaker. If you do not wish to quote a whole statement, it is necessary to indicate those parts you are leaving out by inserting ellipses. (See example on page 58.)

If your quotation is very long it must be separated from the sentences that precede and follow it. It should be indented ten or more spaces and appear in single-spaced type. Do not surround it with quotation marks.

[6] See footnote 5.

Short quotation example:
The early settlers were not hostile to the Indians. As pointed out by the Claxton Banner in 1836: "Our Sioux neighbors, despite their fierce reputation, are a friendly and peaceable people."

Short quotation example with omission:
As pointed out by the Claxton Banner in 1836: "Our Sioux neighbors . . . are a friendly and peaceable people."

Long quotation example:
The early settlers were not hostile to the Indians. As pointed out by the Claxton Banner in 1836:

> Our Sioux neighbors, despite their fierce reputation, are a friendly and peaceable people. No livestock have been disturbed, and the outermost cabins are unmolested. We trust in God that our two peoples may live in harmony in this territory.

It is also possible to insert quoted material in the middle of a sentence (for example, The Prime Minister favored the proposal, but the Foreign Secretary felt it to be "a most dangerous course to pursue," and urged its rejection). In most cases like this, however, a paraphrase is preferable to a quotation. (The Prime Minister favored the proposal, but the Foreign Secretary considered it dangerous and urged its rejection.) Whether you choose to quote or paraphrase, all such references must be footnoted.[7]

Organizing a Bibliography
A bibliography is a listing of the sources you used in writing your paper.[8] The list should appear on a separate page or pages at the end of the paper. If the bibliography is long, say

[7] If a portion of the material you are quoting is in italics (e.g., *New York Times*), you should underline these words when you type them (e.g., New York Times).

[8] It must include all those sources that appear in footnotes. Beyond that, add those works that were important parts of your research. You need not list every source you looked at in the course of your research. Don't pad the bibliography just to make it look more impressive.

more than twenty sources, it should be divided into three categories: (1) primary sources and documents, (2) books, and (3) articles. The sources are listed alphabetically according to the last name of the author. The form for a book is

Link, Arthur S. Woodrow Wilson and the Progressive Era. New York: Harper and Row, 1954.

1. Author, last name first, followed by a period.
2. Title of work, underlined, followed by a period.
3. Place of publication, followed by a colon.
4. Publisher, followed by a comma.
5. Date of publication, followed by a period.

The form for articles is

Bettman, Irwin. "The Beet Sugar Industry: A Study in Tariff Protection," Harvard Business Review, XI (April, 1933), pp. 369–378.

1. Author, last name first, followed by a period.
2. Title of article, followed by a comma, all in quotation marks.
3. Name of the periodical, underlined, followed by a comma.
4. Volume number, followed by date in parenthesis, followed by a comma.
5. Pages on which the article begins and ends, followed by a period.

If there is more than one author, the citation is alphabetized according to the last name of the first author mentioned on the title page of the work. That name is then followed by *all* the others, again with last names first. If there is more than one work by a particular author, only the first listing in the bibliography carries the author's name. All the rest begin with an eight-space underline in place of the name. As with footnotes, if the author is the translator or editor, or if there is more than one volume, these must be noted. If a book is anonymous, it is listed in alphabetical order, by its title. If an article has no author, it is listed, in alphabetical order, by the title of the article. If you have used many volumes of a particular periodical or many issues of a particular newspaper, you need not list each one separately in your bibliography.

They should appear, listed by the name of the periodical or newspaper, as follows:

Monthly Labor Review. Vols. XL–LXX. Washington: United States Bureau of Labor Statistics, 1940–1957.
New York Times. 1954–1958.

The rules governing bibliographical citations for primary documents can be complicated. The best system is to copy the information exactly as it appears in the card catalog.

Revising and Rewriting

Leave time for revising your paper. The process of putting together the research and writing of a history paper is complex, and your first draft will need smoothing out. As you prepare the final draft, check your paper for the following: (1) Does the paper have thematic unity and do its parts follow one from the other? (2) Is there adequate support for the major assertions of fact and interpretation? (3) Are the points made clearly and forcefully? You must also check the mechanics of your paper, especially spelling and grammar. If your paper is typewritten, check for typographical errors, and make all corrections cleanly and clearly. Reading the paper aloud will help you to catch poor sentence construction and awkward phrases.

Preparing your final draft also involves knowledge of the rules of typing style. Make sure that all pages are numbered consecutively, that the sections or chapters are clearly delineated, and that the footnotes and bibliography are clearly separated from the text and neatly organized. If your paper contains additional material such as appendices, graphs, charts, drawings, photographs, or maps, these too must be clearly labeled and separated from the text. If there are many such materials, your paper should contain a table of contents that lists them. Last of all, choose a title for your paper—one that clearly and accurately reflects its contents.

appendix *A*

Basic Reference Sources for History Study and Research

This appendix can be used as a supplement to the reference collection of your school library.[1] To aid you in your research the sources are separated according to the kind of information they contain, and where appropriate, they are organized according to area or subject. This should be of particular value in locating sources at the very beginning of your study of a particular subject. If you have no initial leads on relevant material, or if you are unsatisfied with the sources you have uncovered, the works listed here may enable you to find pertinent facts and historical works.

The reference sources cited here are specially designed for historical research. There are two kinds of works listed: ref-

[1] For information on how to use reference sources in the library see pages 47–52.

erence books, which contain summary or statistical historical information and bibliographies, which contain lists of historical works on particular periods or subjects. Reference books (dictionaries, encyclopedias, biography collections, etc.) are useful for obtaining specific facts or for organizing a general outline of your subject. Bibliographies do not themselves contain historical information but rather are collections of history works on a particular topic.

The purpose of this appendix is to facilitate your search for relevant historical facts and history books. Because it is organized with the needs of the beginning student in mind, it may be easier to use than the reference catalog in your school library. It is therefore a good place to *begin* your research. However, as stated before, it is meant as a *supplement* rather than as a substitute for your library's reference catalog. Many of the works cited here should be available in a good college or public library, but some of them, particularly the specialized bibliographies, may not be. If there is a book listed here that you feel is most valuable for your research and it is not in your library's reference catalog, you will have to try another library or find a comparable work that your library does possess. On the other hand, if your school or public library is a large one, there will be many more sources in its reference catalog than are listed in this chapter, and you should treat these listings as only a first step in your research.

Within each group of sources, those that should be found in most library reference collections or that are particularly useful to beginning students are designated by an asterisk. Those without the asterisk are works less likely to be available at smaller libraries and are generally designed for the use of advanced students and professionals. If any of the latter should be available, however, you may find them valuable in your research.[2]

[2] The books in this appendix are listed by title first so that you can easily sight the work that seems closest to your topic. Following the title is the publication information and then the name of the editor or compiler. When looking up these works in your school or public library's reference catalog, check first under the name of the editor or compiler. If the book is not listed there, it may be filed by the name of the publisher or the title of the work. Where there is more than one edition of a work, use the most recent one available.

1. DICTIONARIES, ENCYCLOPEDIAS, ATLASES, YEARBOOKS, ETC.

These books are general reference works. They can help you to define and correctly spell important terms, gather general information on a particular subject, locate geographical areas, obtain statistical data, and much more. These sources are a good point at which to begin any historical investigation or to consult for a specific fact. However, they do not contain serious developments or interpretations of historical subjects, and therefore should not be depended upon for the substance of your work.

A. GENERAL DICTIONARIES

Oxford English Dictionary. Oxford: Clarendon Press, 1888–1928. James A. H. Murray et al., eds. "A New English Dictionary on Historical Principles." This dictionary is the most complete English-language dictionary. If you are studying the historical development of the meaning of a word it is an essential reference. If, however, your concern is to determine the contemporary spelling or definition of a term, the following dictionaries are better sources. They are unabridged language dictionaries. If the term you are searching for is colloquial or is a recent derivation, be sure to use the most recent edition available.

* *Webster's New International Dictionary*
* *Funk and Wagnall's New Standard Dictionary*
* *The Random House Dictionary of the American Language*

B. HISTORICAL DICTIONARIES

These dictionaries define only historical terms. Unlike language dictionaries, they also give a brief general description of the origin and general historical context of the term. Some have quite extensive explanations of historical terms and thus are similar to encyclopedias.

* *Webster's Guide to American History.* Springfield, Mass.: G. and C. Merriam, 1971.
* *Concise Dictionary of American History.* New York: Charles Scribner's Sons, 1962. Thomas C. Cochran and Wayne Andrews, eds.

An Encyclopedic Dictionary of American History. New York: Washington Square Press, 1968. Howard Hurwitz, ed.

Dictionary of American History. New York: Charles Scribner's Sons, 1942–1961. James T. Adams, ed. (Revised edition in preparation.) This is the most extensive dictionary of American history, but it is an older publication and some school libraries may not have it. The best substitute is *Concise Dictionary of American History,* listed above.

Concise Dictionary of Ancient History. New York: Philosophical Society, 1955. Percival Woodcock, ed.

Dictionary of European History. New York: Philosophical Library, 1954. William S. Roeder, ed.

A Dictionary of British History. New York: St. Martin's Press, 1970. Sigfrid H. Steinberg, ed.

C. SOCIAL SCIENCE DICTIONARIES

Dictionary of Social Science. Washington, D.C.: Public Affairs Press, 1959. John T. Zadrozny, ed.

White's Political Dictionary. New York: World Publishing Company, 1947. Wilbur W. White, ed.

D. GENERAL ENCYCLOPEDIAS

* *Encyclopedia Britannica.* Chicago: Encyclopedia Britannica Corporation, 1970. This is one of the best encyclopedias. If your subject is a recent one, or if important new facts and interpretations have arisen in recent years, be sure to obtain the latest edition of whatever encyclopedia you use. If a recent edition is not available, check the annual supplements published by most good encyclopedias.

* *Encyclopedia Americana.* New York: The Americana Corporation.

* *Collier's Encyclopedia.* New York: Crowell Collier and Macmillan.

Compton's Pictured Encyclopedia and Fact-Index. Chicago: Encyclopedia Britannica, Inc.

E. HISTORICAL ENCYCLOPEDIAS

* *An Encyclopedia of World History, Ancient, Medieval and Modern, Chronologically Arranged.* Boston: Houghton Mifflin Company, 1972. William L. Langer, ed.

* *Harper Encyclopedia of the Modern World* [1760 to present]. New York: Harper & Row, 1970. Richard B. Morris and Graham W. Irwin, eds.
* *Encyclopedia of American History.* New York: Harper & Row, 1970. Richard B. Morris, ed.

F. SOCIAL SCIENCE AND SPECIALIZED ENCYCLOPEDIAS

* *International Encyclopedia of the Social Sciences.* New York: Macmillan, 1968. David L. Sills, ed. If your research takes you into such fields as political science, economics, anthropology, law, sociology, and psychology, this is an important source book for you. An earlier work, *Encyclopedia of the Social Sciences,* New York, Macmillan, 1930–1934, edited by Edwin R. A. Seligman and Alvin Johnson, is also valuable for such subjects, although it is now out of date.

Encyclopedia of Philosophy. New York: Macmillan, 1966. Paul Edwards, ed.

The International Jewish Encyclopedia. Englewood Cliffs, N.J.: Prentice-Hall, 1973. Ben Isaacson and Deborah Wigoder, eds.

G. GENERAL ATLASES

The Times Atlas of the World. London: Times Publishing Company, 1955–1959. John Bartholomew, ed. Vol. I—World, Australia, East Asia; Vol. II—India, Middle East, Russia; Vol. III—Northern Europe; Vol. IV—Mediterranean and Africa; Vol. V—Americas.

* *Cosmopolitan World Atlas.* Chicago: Rand McNally & Co., 1959.

Oxford Economic Atlas of the World. Oxford: Oxford University Press, 1972.

* *Webster's Geographical Dictionary.* Springfield, Mass.: G. and C. Merriam. This source is not useful for map reference, but is a convenient source for determining the spelling, location, and description of geographical terms.

H. HISTORICAL ATLASES

Historical Atlas. New York: Barnes & Noble, 1956. William R. Shepherd, ed.

Historical Atlas of World History. Chicago: Rand McNally, 1961. Robert R. Palmer et al., eds.

* *Historical Atlas of the United States.* New York: Henry Holt & Company, 1953. Clifford L. Lord and Elizabeth H. Lord, eds.

Atlas of the Classical World. New York: Thomas Nelson & Sons, 1959. A. A. M. van der Heyden and H. H. Scullard, eds.

Muir's Atlas of Ancient and Classical History. New York: Barnes & Noble, 1961.

* *Muir's Historical Atlas: Ancient, Medieval & Modern.* New York: Barnes & Noble, 1962.

Atlas of European History. New York: Oxford University Press, 1957. Edward W. Fox and H. S. Deighton, eds.

Atlas of World History. Chicago: Rand McNally, 1957. Robert R. Palmer et al., eds.

I. YEARBOOKS

* *Statesman's Yearbook.* New York: Macmillan, 1864–present. This and the following yearbooks provide up-to-date political information, especially of a governmental nature.

Political Handbook of the World. New York: Harper & Row, 1927–present. Council on Foreign Relations. Walter H. Mallory, ed.

United Nations Statistical Yearbook. New York: United Nations Statistical Office, 1949–present. There is also a *United Nations Demographic Yearbook,* which provides world and national population statistics.

2. BIOGRAPHY COLLECTIONS

These works are collections of short biographies of well-known persons. They contain a general outline of the milestones and accomplishments of individuals who are considered to have made notable contributions to the times in which they lived and/or to posterity. These works are useful as a first step in biographical research on persons central to your topic or as a way of identifying characters peripheral to it. Each collection has different criteria for determining which individuals it includes. Take care to select the biography collection that is most likely to include the type of individual on whom you are seeking information.

A. GUIDES TO BIOGRAPHY COLLECTIONS

Biographical Information: Where to Find It. Detroit: Gale Research Company, n.d.

* *Biography Index: A Cumulative Guide to Biographical Material in Books and Magazines.* New York: H. W. Wilson Company, 1949–present.

B. BRITISH BIOGRAPHY COLLECTIONS

* *Dictionary of National Biography.* Oxford: Oxford University Press, 1922. Leslie Stephan and Sidney Lee, eds. Supplement, Boston: G. K. Hall, 1966.

Who's Who. London: Allen & Unwin, 1849–present. Annual. This volume covers *living* individuals. For historical research, you must choose a year during which your subject was most active, or preferably use the *Who Was Who* collection, which follows.

Who Was Who. Vol. I, 1897–1915; Vol. II, 1916–1928; Vol. III, 1929–1940; Vol. IV, 1941–1950. (See annotation to *Who Was Who in America* for further information.)

C. AMERICAN BIOGRAPHY COLLECTIONS

* *Dictionary of American Biography.* New York: Charles Scribner's Sons, 1928–1958, including supplements. This is the best source for biographies of historical personages of the United States. It includes both U.S. citizens and people who lived much of their lives in this country even if they were not citizens. It lists only individuals who are no longer living. As with most biography collections, the date of original publication is the best key to determining who is included. Most of these volumes were written between 1928 and 1936. If your subject died after 1928, check the supplements. Supplement I covers deaths up through the end of 1935; supplement II, 1940; supplement III, 1945.

National Cyclopedia of American Biography. Ann Arbor: University Microfilms, 1967. Unlike the *Dictionary of Amer-*

ican Biography, this is not an alphabetical listing, but it does have an alphabetical index at the end of each volume. This collection is published in two series: a "Current" series and a "Permanent" series. The Permanent series includes only individuals no longer living at date of publication for the volume in which they were to be included. Although this work was reprinted in 1967, the original volumes of the Permanent series were written in the 1890s. If your subject was living in the twentieth century, consult the Current series, which includes only persons living at date of publication.

Who's Who in America. Chicago: Marquis Who's Who, 1897–present. This volume covers living individuals. For purposes of historical research you must obtain the older volumes, or preferably, use the *Who Was Who* collections that follow.

Who Was Who in America. Vol. I, 1897–1942; Vol. II, 1943–1950; Vol. III, 1951–1960. Chicago: Marquis Who's Who, 1943, 1950, 1962. The years covered in each volume indicate the dates of death for those included. For example, if your subject died in 1945, he/she should be included in Vol. II. For individuals who died before 1897, see *Who Was Who in America: Historical Volume, 1607–1896.*

* *Who Was Who in America: Historical Volume, 1607–1896.* Chicago: Marquis Who's Who, 1963.

Biographical Directory of the American Congress, 1774–1961. Washington, D.C.: Government Printing Office, 1961.

Biographic Register [of the United States State Department]. Washington, D.C.: Government Printing Office, 1869–present. This is an annual volume, and you must choose a year during which your subject served in the State Department.

Biographic Dictionary of the United States Executive, 1774–1971. Westport, Conn.: Greenwood, 1971.

Who's Who of American Women. Chicago: Marquis Who's Who, 1973.

D. INTERNATIONAL BIOGRAPHY COLLECTIONS

These collections list persons of all national origins.

* *Current Biography.* New York: H. W. Wilson Co., 1940–

present. This covers living persons. Older volumes, how-
ever, may list individuals who are now of historical signifi-
cance. Only useful for historical research for the period
since the 1930s. To locate the volume you need check
Current Biography: Cumulated Index, 1940–1970.
° *Webster's Biographical Dictionary.* Springfield, Mass.: G.
and C. Merriam.
International Who's Who. London: Europa, 1935–present.
New York Times Obituary Index, 1858–1968. New York: New
York Times, 1970.
Encyclopedia of World Biography. New York: McGraw-Hill,
1973. David I. Eggenberger, ed.

E. NATIONAL BIOGRAPHY COLLECTIONS

Most national biography collections, except for the United
Kingdom and the United States, which are covered separately,
deal with contemporary personages. However, they may be
useful for research into recent history or for obtaining information on the early careers of contemporary figures. Here
is a brief selection.

Dictionary of Canadian Biography. Toronto: University of
Toronto Press, 1966–present.
Who's Who in Latin America. Chicago: A. N. Marquis Co.,
1946–1951. Percy A. Martin, ed.
Who's Who in Communist China. Hong Kong: Union Re-
search Institute, 1966.
Who's Who in the Union of Soviet Socialist Republics. New
York: Scarecrow Press, 1966.

F. SPECIALIZED BIOGRAPHY COLLECTIONS

A Bibliography of American Autobiographies. Madison: Uni-
versity of Wisconsin Press, 1961. Louis Kaplan et al.,
comps.
American Men and Women of Science. New York: Bowker,
1906–present.
Directory of American Scholars. New York: Bowker. American
Council of Learned Societies.
A Biographical Dictionary of World War II. New York: St.
Martin's Press, 1972. Christopher Tunney, ed.

3. NEWSPAPER DIRECTORIES AND INDEXES

In most cases, the beginning student will have access only to the few newspapers held in his or her school or local public library. If you determine, however, that a particular newspaper is of special importance to you, the best way to locate back issues is to check a newspaper directory. These directories can tell you in which libraries that newspaper can be found and how complete the collection is. Remember, the newspaper directory is of use only if you know the name of the particular paper for which you are looking. Moreover, unless you have easy access to a large university or public library, most of the newspapers in a directory will be located far from your school. You might be able to obtain the newspapers you need if they are on microfilm, but this can take several weeks. In most cases, it is best to confine yourself to the newspaper collections in nearby libraries.

A. NEWSPAPER DIRECTORIES

American Newspapers, 1821–1936: A Union List of Files Available in the United States and Canada. New York: H. W. Wilson, 1937. Winifred Gerould, ed.

Newspapers on Microfilm: A Union Check List. Washington, D.C.: Library of Congress, 1963. George Schwegman, Jr., ed.

African Newspapers in Selected American Libraries. Washington, D.C.: Library of Congress, 1962.

Latin American Newspapers in United States Libraries. Austin: University of Texas Press, 1969. Steven M. Charno, ed.

B. NEWSPAPER INDEXES

Once you know that you have access to a particular newspaper, you must determine which issues contain articles on your subject. If your subject is a specific event, then merely check the issues of the newspaper published at the time or shortly after the event. However, if you are seeking articles about an event that was not confined to a particular day or week (for example, the stock market crash of 1929), then you will have to check newspaper issues covering many weeks or even months. An indispensable aid in such a task is the newspaper index.

If you know the year in which the event occurred, then a newspaper index can tell you the days in that year when a particular paper contained articles or editorials on your subject. Because the index saves you the trouble of reading each issue, it is indispensable for research into events that were not limited to a brief period. The only problem with newspaper indexes is that there are so few of them. If there is no index to the paper you wish to read, the best thing to do is to check the index of another newspaper. This will tell you the dates on which that newspaper carried articles on your subject. You can then go back to the newspaper in which you were initially interested and read it for those dates. In most cases you won't be far off.

* *New York Times Index*. New York: New York Times, 1913–present. This is usually the best source for beginning students. Most libraries have files of the *New York Times*, and the index is very complete.

New York Daily Tribune Index. New York: Tribune Association, 1876–1907.

Palmer's Index to The Times [of London] *Newspaper*, 1790–1943. London: 1868–1943.

Official Index to the Times [of London]. London: 1907–present.

Christian Science Monitor Index. Corvallis, Oregon: 1960–present. Because it goes back only to 1960, it is of limited use for historical research.

4. PERIODICAL GUIDES AND INDEXES

Periodical guides describe the general content and location of periodicals. Like newspaper guides, they are most useful if you already know that you want a particular periodical and are seeking information as to where collections of it can be found. If the periodical guide lists no library convenient to you, it is best to check into other periodicals.

A. PERIODICAL GUIDES

* *Union List of Serials in Libraries of the United States and Canada*. New York: H. W. Wilson, 1943.
* *New Serial Titles: A Union List of Serials Commencing Publication after December 31, 1949*. Washington, D.C.:

Library of Congress, 1953–present. If you are seeking a
newer periodical, this guide is the best source.

World List of Historical Periodicals. New York: H. W. Wilson
Co., 1939. Pierre Caron and Marc Jaryc, eds.

*Historical Periodicals: An Annotated World List of Historical
and Related Serial Publications.* Santa Barbara, Cal.: Clio
Press, 1961. Eric H. Boehm and Lalit Adolphus, eds.

Guide to Current Latin American Periodicals. Gainesville,
Fla.: Kallman Publishing Co., 1961. Irene Zimmerman, ed.

B. GENERAL PERIODICAL INDEXES

These works list articles that have appeared in periodical
publications. They are usually organized by subject, and contain all of the articles on a given topic that appeared in the
periodicals that are indexed. The periodicals covered by a
particular index are usually listed at the very beginning of
the volume. When you choose an index be sure that it covers
the kind of periodical likely to contain articles on your subject
and that these articles are written for a serious or scholarly
audience.

*Historical Abstracts, 1775–1945: Bibliography of the World's
Periodical Literature.* Santa Barbara, Cal.: Clio Press,
1955–present. Eric H. Boehm, ed.

* *Reader's Guide to Periodical Literature.* New York: H. W.
Wilson, 1900–present. These volumes cover the twentieth
century. You must be selective when using them because
many of the periodicals they cover are written for a popular rather than a scholarly audience. However, the
magazines listed are valuable as records of popular opinions and interests.

* *Nineteenth Century Reader's Guide to Periodical Literature.*
New York: H. W. Wilson, 1944.

Poole's Index to Periodical Literature, 1802–1881. Boston:
Houghton Mifflin Co., 1891. There is a supplement covering 1882–1906.

* *Social Science and Humanities Index.* New York: H. W. Wilson, 1907–present. This is often the best single guide for
historical researchers.

* *Essay and General Literature Index.* New York: H. W. Wil-

son, 1800–present. This work lists articles published in collections of readings rather than in periodicals.
* *Public Affairs Information Service Bulletin.* New York: P.A.I.S., 1915–present. This work emphasizes periodicals and other publications in the social sciences and includes many government publications.

C. SPECIALIZED PERIODICAL INDEXES

There are many periodical indexes on specialized topics. If your research takes you into these specialized fields, the indexes listed here may be worth looking into.

Agricultural Index; Applied Science and Technology Index; Art Index; Business Periodicals Index; Education Index; Index to Legal Periodicals; Index Medicus. (All are published by the H. W. Wilson Company of New York.)

Some specialized periodical indexes of value in historical research are

Women's Magazines 1693–1968. London: Michael Joseph, 1970. Cynthia White, comp.
From Radical Left to Extreme Right. Ann Arbor: Campus Publishers, 1970–present. Robert H. Muller, et al. This index covers periodicals of dissent and protest.
* *American Historical Review: General Index for Volumes XLI–LX, 1935–1955.* New York: Macmillan, 1962.
* *Guide to the American Historical Review, 1895–1945.* Washington, D.C.: Government Printing Office, 1945. Franklin D. Scott and Elaine Tegler, comps. (This work is to be found in American Historical Association, *Annual Report for the Year 1944,* Vol. I, pt. 2, pp. 65–292.)
Foreign Affairs 50-Year Index: Vols. 1–50, 1922–1972. New York: Council on Foreign Relations, 1973. Robt. J. Palmer, comp.

5. HISTORICAL PERIODICALS

This is a brief list of some of the best-known historical periodicals. These journals specialize in articles on historical subjects and are written for professional and student researchers. Some have their own cumulative indexes (like that to

the *American Historical Review* listed above) and thus can
be useful places to begin the search for historical material.
There are also many specialized periodicals in history. Be
sure to look into those that deal with your topic area.

Current History	*Journal of American History*
Journal of Asian Studies	*Journal of Southern History*
Middle East Journal	*Canadian Historical Review*
Slavic Review	*Hispanic American Historical*
Journal of Economic History	*Review*
English Historical Review	*Journal of Modern History*
American Historical Review	

6. GOVERNMENT PUBLICATIONS AND PUBLIC DOCUMENTS

These works are guides to books, pamphlets, speeches,
treaties, hearings, reports, etc., published by public agencies.
This list, like all others in this appendix, is confined to works
in English and is by no means complete. If your research topic
is related to governmental affairs at any level, these works
can lead you to documents and publications by or about the
agencies you are studying. The major publications of the
U.S. government are available at many libraries.

A. INTERNATIONAL AGENCIES

*Guide to League of Nations Publications: A Bibliographical
Survey of the Work of the League, 1920–1947.* New York:
Columbia University Press, 1951. Hans Aufricht, comp.
United Nations Documents Index. New York: United Nations
Library, 1950–present. This volume is issued annually.

B. FOREIGN GOVERNMENT PUBLICATIONS

*Manual of Government Publications, United States and For-
eign.* New York: Appleton Century Crofts, 1950. Everette
S. Brown, comp.
Great Britain, Parliament: Parliamentary Debates. London:
1803–present.

C. UNITED STATES GOVERNMENT PUBLICATIONS

United States Government Publications. New York: H. W.
Wilson, 1949. Anne Boyd, comp.

Subject Guide to United States Government Publications. Chicago: American Library Association, 1947. Herbert Hirshberg and Carl Melinat, comps.

* *A Popular Guide to Government Publications.* New York: Columbia University Press, 1968. William P. Leidy, comp.

* *Subject Guide to Major United States Government Publications.* Chicago: American Library Association, 1968. Ellen P. Jackson, comp.

Monthly Catalogue of United States Government Publications. Washington, D.C.: Government Printing Office, 1895–present.

Checklist of United States Public Documents, 1789–1909. Washington, D.C.: Government Printing Office, 1911, and J. W. Edwards, 1958.

Catalogue of Public Documents of the United States, 1893–1940. Washington, D.C.: Government Printing Office, 1895–1945.

Congressional Record: United States Congress. Washington, D.C.: Government Printing Office, 1873–present.

Government Publications and Their Use. Washington, D.C.: Brookings Institute, 1961. Laurence Schmeckebier and Roy Eastin, eds.

Subject Guide to Government Reference Books. Littleton, Colo.: Libraries Unlimited, 1972. Sally Wynkoop, ed.

D. STATE AND LOCAL GOVERNMENT PUBLICATIONS

State Publications: A Provisional List of Official Publications of the Several States of the United States. New York: Publishers Weekly, 1908. Richard R. Bowker.

Bibliography of County Histories of the 3,111 Counties in the United States. Baltimore: Clarence Peterson, 1946.

For the publications of the state historical societies, see the list of these societies in Appendix B.

7. SUBJECT BIBLIOGRAPHIES

A subject bibliography lists printed works on a particular topic. The ones listed here have been chosen with a preference for those that the beginning student is likely to be able to obtain. In this regard, emphasis has been placed on bibliographies that are written especially for students, are of recent publication or republication and therefore likely to have entered new library collections, contain predominantly or solely works in the English language, and are general rather than specialized. Those that are especially useful to beginning students have been designated by an asterisk (*).[3]

A. DISCIPLINES OTHER THAN HISTORY

These bibliographies list works in fields other than history. If an important aspect of your research topic falls under other major branches of knowledge, then valuable materials may exist in nonhistorical publications.

Bibliographies: Subject and National. New York: Hafner, 1962. Robert L. Collison, ed. This is a bibliography of bibliographies.

* A *Select Bibliography: Asia, Africa, Eastern Europe, Latin America.* New York: American University, 1960, plus supplements. These are studies in the social sciences covering the developing countries of the world. For more recent works see *Cumulative Supplement, 1961–1971.*

Ethnographic Bibliography of North America. New Haven: Human Relations Area Files, 1959. George P. Murdock, ed.

Sources of Information in the Social Sciences. Totowa, N.J.: Bedminster Press, 1964. Carl M. White, ed.

An Interdisciplinary Bibliography on Nationalism, 1935–1953. Cambridge: Massachusetts Institute of Technology Press, 1956. Karl W. Deutsch, ed.

Books on Communism: A Bibliography. London: Ampersand Ltd., 1959. Robert N. Carew Hunt, ed.

Handbook in the History of Philosophy. New York: Barnes & Noble, 1961.

B. GENERAL HISTORY

The remainder of this appendix contains the basic source material for historical research—history bibliographies. Once you have chosen your research topic, these bibliographies and

[3] If the title of a bibliography indicates that it is annotated, this means that it not only *lists* books on a particular topic but also provides a brief description of their contents.

the reference catalog of your library should be your initial step in finding sources on that topic. For convenience to the beginning student, the list of subject bibliographies is separated according to the chronological period or geographical area that the works cover. The bibliographies themselves break down the topics even further.

Don't expect to find an entire bibliography dedicated to your particular subject. Choose the ones that cover the period or area into which your own topic falls. Remember, your library will probably not have all of these books. If the most promising bibliography is not there, try a different work.

* *American Historical Association: Guide to Historical Literature.* New York: Macmillan, 1961. George F. Howe et al., eds.

Historical Bibliographies. New York: Russell, 1965. Edith M. Coulter and Melanie Gerstenfeld, eds.

Books for College Libraries. Chicago: American Library Association, 1967. Melvin Voigt and Joseph Treyz, comps. Both bibliographies and historical works are listed by subject on pages 92–261.

International Bibliography of Historical Sciences. New York: H. W. Wilson, 1926–1949.

Reference Works: History and Related Fields. Santa Barbara, Cal.: ABC-Clio, 1967. Inge Boehm and Alexander Birkos, eds.

* *World Historical Fiction Guide.* Metuchen, N.J.: Scarecrow Press, 1973. Daniel McGarry and Sarah White, eds. If you are studying historical novels, this is an important source.

Books on World History: A Guide for Teachers and Students. University of Indiana Press, 1973. Warren Wagar, ed.

Bibliography of the History of Technology. Cambridge, Mass.: M.I.T. Press, 1968. Eugene S. Ferguson, ed.

* *A Reader's Guide to Contemporary History.* Chicago: Quadrangle Books, 1972. Bernard Krikler and Walter Laqueur, eds.

C. ANCIENT HISTORY

* *Introduction to Ancient History.* Berkeley: University of California, 1970. Herman Bengtson.

Oxford Classical Dictionary. Oxford: Clarendon Press, 1970.
N. G. L. Hammond and H. H. Scullard, eds.

International Guide to Classical Studies. Darien, Conn.: American Bibliographic Service, 1958–present. Annual.

The Ancient World. New York: Harper Bros., 1950. Joseph W. Swain. This book is itself a historical work, but it is listed here because of its valuable bibliography.

The Cambridge Ancient History. London: Cambridge University Press, 1970–present. This is a multivolume historical work with extensive bibliographies.

D. MEDIEVAL HISTORY

* *A Guide to the Study of Medieval History.* New York: F. S.. Crofts & Sons, 1931. Louis J. Paetow. This guide is updated in a supplement by Gray C. Boyce, Medieval Academy of America, 1962.

International Guide to Medieval Studies. Darien, Conn.: American Bibliographic Service, 1958–present. Annual.

Reference Studies in Medieval History. Chicago: University of Chicago Press, 1925–1930. James W. Thompson.

History of the Byzantine Empire, 324–1453. Madison: University of Wisconsin Press, 1952. Alexander Vasiliev. Listed here because of its good bibliography.

Medieval European History, 395–1500: A Select Bibliography. London: Philip, 1955. Historical Association of London.

Cambridge Medieval History. Cambridge: Cambridge University Press, 1911–1936.

Who's Who in the Middle Ages. New York: Stein and Day, 1970. John Fines, ed.

E. MODERN EUROPEAN HISTORY

Select List of Works on Europe and Europe Overseas, 1715–1815. Oxford: Clarendon Press, 1956. John Bromley and A. Goodwin, eds.

Select List of Books on European History, 1815–1914. Oxford: Clarendon Press, 1957. Alan Bullock and A. J. P. Taylor, eds.

Bibliography for the Study of European History, 1815–1939. Ann Arbor: Edwards Bros., 1942. With supplements. Lowell J. Ragatz, ed.

* *Cambridge Modern History.* Cambridge: Cambridge University Press, 1957–present. These history volumes have large bibliographies. *The New Cambridge Modern History,* however, has no bibliography.
* *A History of the Modern World.* New York: Knopf, 1950. Robert R. Palmer. Another history work with an extensive bibliography.

F. ENGLISH HISTORY

Sources and Literature of English History from the Earliest Times to About 1485. London: Longmans Green, 1915. Charles Gross, ed. This work has been revised by the American Historical Association under the editorship of Edgar B. Greaves.

An Anglo-Saxon and Celtic Bibliography, 450–1087. Oxford: Blackwell, 1957. Welfrid Bonser, ed.

Bibliography of British History: Tudor Period, 1485–1603. Oxford: Clarendon Press, 1959. Conyers Read, ed.

Bibliography of British History: Stuart Period, 1603–1714. Oxford: Clarendon Press, 1928. Godfrey Davies, ed. This work has been revised by the American Historical Association, edited by Mary F. Keeler, New York: Oxford University Press, 1970.

Bibliography of British History: The Eighteenth Century 1714–1789. Oxford: Clarendon Press, 1951. Stanley Pargellis and D. J. Medley, eds. Other volumes in this series cover 1789–1851 and 1855–1914.

* *Writings on British History: A Bibliography of Books and Articles on the History of Great Britain from about 450 to 1914.* New York: Barnes & Noble, 1937–1961. A. T. Milne, ed.

* *Oxford History of England,* Vol. 15, 1914–1945. Oxford: Clarendon Press, 1965. A. J. P. Taylor, ed. See bibliography at end of volume.

G. SCOTTISH HISTORY

A Bibliography of Works Related to Scotland, 1916–1950. Edinburgh: University Press, 1959–1960. P. D. Hancock, ed.

H. IRISH HISTORY

Encyclopedia of Ireland. Dublin: Allen Figgis, 1968.
Guide to Irish Bibliographical Material. London: Library Association, 1964. Alan R. Eager, ed.

I. BRITISH EMPIRE HISTORY

Cambridge History of the British Empire. Cambridge: Cambridge University Press, 1929–1959. John Rose, Arthur Newton, and Ernest Benians, eds. Bibliographies at the end of each of eight volumes.

J. CANADIAN HISTORY

A Checklist of Canadian Literature and Background Material, 1628–1950. Toronto: University of Toronto Press, 1959. Reginald Walters, ed.
Bibliography of Canadian Bibliographies. Toronto: University of Toronto Press, 1960. Raymond Tanghe, ed.
Encyclopedia Canadiana. Toronto: Grolier, 1972.

K. EAST EUROPEAN HISTORY

Handbook of Slavic Studies. Cambridge, Mass.: Harvard University Press, 1949. Leonid Strakhovsky, ed.
* *The Balkans Since 1453.* New York: Rinehart, 1958. Leften S. Stavrianos. There is an extensive bibliography at the end of this work.
Bibliography of American Publications on East Central Europe 1945–1957. Bloomington: Indiana University Press, 1958. Robert F. Byrnes, ed.
Cambridge History of Poland. Cambridge: Cambridge University Press, 1941–1950. See the bibliography in Vol. III.

L. RUSSIAN HISTORY (AND USSR)

Junior Slavica: A Selected, Annotated Bibliography of Books in English on Russia and Eastern Europe. Rochester, N.Y.: Libraries Unlimited, 1968. Stephan M. Horak, ed.
Guide to Research in Russian History. Syracuse, N.Y.: Syracuse University Press, 1951. Charles Morley, ed.
Guide to Russian Reference Books. Stanford, Cal.: Hoover Institution, 1962. Karol Maichel et al., eds.

* *A Select Bibliography of Works in English on Russian History, 1801–1917.* Oxford: Blackwell, 1962. David Shapiro, ed.
* *Encyclopedia of Russia and the Soviet Union.* New York: McGraw Hill, 1961. Michael T. Florinsky, ed.
* *A History of Soviet Russia.* London: Macmillan, 1950–1960. Edward H. Carr. See bibliography at end of work.
Historical Atlas of the U.S.S.R. New York: C. S. Hammond, 1950.
An Atlas of Russian History. New Haven, Conn.: Yale University Press, 1970. Allen F. Chew, ed.
Russia and the Soviet Union: A Bibliographic Guide to Western Language Publications. Chicago: University of Chicago Press, 1965. Paul Horecky, ed.

M. AFRICAN HISTORY [4]

Introduction to Africa: A Selective Guide to Background Reading. Washington, D.C.: University Press of Washington, 1952. Library of Congress.
* *A Selected Bibliography on Traditional and Modern Africa.* Syracuse, N.Y.: Syracuse University Press, 1968. Peter Gutkind and John B. Webster, eds.
African Affairs for the General Reader: A Selected and Introductory Bibliographic Guide. New York: Council of the African-American Institute, 1967. African Bibliographic Center.
Current Themes in African Historical Studies: A Selected Bibliographical Guide to Resources for Research in African History. Westport, Conn.: Negro Universities Press, 1970. Daniel G. Matthews, ed.
Africa South of the Sahara: A Selected, Annotated List of Writings, 1951–1956. Washington, D.C.: Library of Congress, 1957. Library of Congress, General Reference and Bibliography Division.
Africa South of the Sahara: A Select and Annotated Bibliography, 1964–1968. Stanford, Cal.: Hoover Institution Press, 1969. Kenneth Glazier, ed.
* *Guide to Research and Reference Works on Sub-Saharan*

[4] For the northern African states that border on the Mediterranean, see Near and Middle Eastern History.

Africa. Stanford, Cal.: Hoover Institution Press, 1971.
Peter Duigman, ed.

Selected Annotated Bibliography of Tropical Africa. New
York: International African Institute, 1956. Daryll Ford,
comp.

African Newspapers in Selected American Libraries. Washington, D.C.: Library of Congress, 1962.

Atlas of African History. London: E. Arnold, 1958. J. D. Fage,
ed.

N. NEAR AND MIDDLE EASTERN HISTORY

* *The Near and Middle East: An Introduction to History and
Bibliography.* Washington, D.C.: American Historical Association, 1959. Roderic H. Davidson, ed.

Concise Encyclopedia of the Middle East. Washington, D.C.:
Public Affairs Press, 1973. Mehdi Heravi, ed.

The Arabian Peninsula: A Selected, Annotated List of Periodicals, Books and Articles in English. Washington, D.C.:
Library of Congress, 1951.

Handbook and Annotated Bibliographies [on the Arab countries, Iran, and Afghanistan]. New Haven: Human Relations Area Files Press, 1956.

* *A Short History of the Middle East from the Rise of Islam
to Modern Times.* New York: Praeger, 1957. George E.
Kirk. See bibliography at end of volume.

* *Concise Encyclopedia of Arabic Civilizations: The Arab
East.* New York: Praeger, 1959. Stephan and Nandy
Ronart, eds.

Who's Who in the Arab World. Beirut: Editions Publitec, 1967–
present. Biennial editions. Useful only for recent history.

Atlas of Islamic History. Princeton: Princeton University Press,
1954. Harry W. Hazard, ed.

* *Books on Asia from the Near East to the Far East: A Guide
for General Readers.* Toronto: University of Toronto, 1971.
Eleazir Birnbaum, ed.

O. GENERAL ASIAN HISTORY

Cumulative Bibliography of Asian Studies, 1941–1965. Boston:
G. K. Hall, 1970.

East Asia: A Bibliography for Undergraduate Libraries. Williamsport, Pa.: Bro-Dart, 1970. Donald G. Gillian et al., eds. This book is written for librarians, but can be used by students as well.

* *Introduction to Asia: A Selective Guide to Background Reading.* Washington, D.C.: Library of Congress, 1955. Quan Lau-king, ed.

Handbook of Oriental History. London: Royal Historical Society, 1951. London University, School of Oriental and African Studies.

Islands of the Pacific: A Selected List of References. Washington, D.C.: Library of Congress, 1943. Library of Congress, General Reference and Bibliography Division.

Outline Atlas of Eastern History. London: Edward Arnold, 1954. Roger R. Sellman, ed.

* *Books on Asia from the Near East to the Far East: A Guide for General Readers.* Toronto: University of Toronto Press, 1971. Eleazir Birnbaum, ed.

Oriental and Asian Bibliography. Hamden, Conn.: Archon, 1966. J. D. Pearson, ed.

P. ASIAN HISTORY—INDIA, PAKISTAN, CEYLON

* *India: A Critical Bibliography.* Tucson: University of Arizona Press, 1964. J. Michael Mahar, ed.

A *Dictionary of Indian History.* New York: Braziler, 1967. Sachchidananda Bhattacharya.

* *The History of India: Its Study and Interpretation.* Washington, D.C.: American Historical Association, 1958. Robert D. Crane.

Introduction to the Civilization of India: Handbook. Chicago: University of Chicago Press, 1961.

* *Cambridge History of India.* New York: Macmillan, 1968. See bibliography at end of volume.

An Historical Atlas of the Indian Peninsula. New York: Oxford University Press, 1959. Cuthbert C. Davies, ed.

South Asia: A Selected Bibliography on India, Pakistan and Ceylon. American Institute of Pacific Relations, 1957. Patrick Wilson, ed.

Q. ASIAN HISTORY—SOUTHEAST ASIA

* *Southeast Asia: A Critical Bibliography*. Tucson: University of Arizona Press, 1969. Kennedy G. Tregonning, ed.

* *Southeast Asian History: A Bibliographic Guide*. New York: Praeger, 1962. Stephen Hay and Margaret Case, eds.

A Guide to Books on Southeast Asian History [1961–1966]. Santa Barbara, Cal.: A.B.C.-Clio, 1969. Gayle Morrison, comp.

Southeast Asia: An Annotated Bibliography. New York: Greenwood Press, 1968. Cecil C. Hobbs, ed.

Vietnam: A Comprehensive Bibliography. Metuchen, N.J.: Scarecrow Press, 1973. John H. M. Chen, ed.

R. ASIAN HISTORY—CHINA

* *China: A Critical Bibliography*. Tucson: University of Arizona, 1962. Charles O. Hucker, ed.

* *Chinese History: A Bibliographical Review*. Washington, D.C.: American Historical Association, 1958. Charles O. Hucker, ed.

Historical Atlas of China. Chicago: Aldine, 1966. Albert Herrmann, ed.

S. ASIAN HISTORY—JAPAN AND KOREA

* *Japanese History: New Dimensions of Approach and Understanding*. Washington, D.C.: American Historical Association, 1961. John W. Hall, ed.

* *Japan and Korea: A Critical Bibliography*. Tucson: University of Arizona Press, 1962. Bernard Silberman, ed.

A Guide to Reference and Research Materials on Korean History: An Annotated Bibliography. Honolulu: East-West Center, 1968. William E. Hentworth, ed.

T. LATIN AMERICAN AND CARIBBEAN HISTORY

Handbook of Latin American Studies. Cambridge, Mass.: Harvard University Press, 1936–1947 and Gainesville: University of Florida Press, 1948–present. Annual volume.

* *Latin America: A Guide to the Historical Literature*. Austin: University of Texas Press, 1971. Charles C. Griffin, ed.

A Guide to Latin American Studies. Los Angeles: University of California, 1967. Martin H. Sable, ed.

* *Latin American History: A Guide to the Literature in English*. New York: Oxford University Press, 1958. R. A. Humphreys, ed.

Latin America and the Caribbean: A Bibliographic Guide to Works in English. Coral Gables: University of Miami Press, 1967. Stojan A. Bayitch, ed.

* *Latin America and the Caribbean: A Handbook*. New York: Praeger, 1968, Claudio Veliz, ed.

Encyclopedia of Latin American History. Indianapolis: Bobbs Merrill, 1968. Michael Martin and Gabriel Lovett.

Who's Who in Latin America. Stanford: Stanford University Press, 1951. Reprinted by Blaine Ethridge Books, Detroit, 1971. Ronald Hilton, ed.

* *Guide to the Hispanic American Historical Review, 1945–1955*. Durham, N.C.: Duke University Press, 1958. Charles Gibson, ed. The years 1918 to 1945 are indexed by Ruth L. Butler.

Index to Latin American Periodical Literature, 1929–1960. New York: G. K. Hall, 1962. Pan American Union.

U. GENERAL UNITED STATES HISTORY

In the case of United States history, the bibliographies have been broken down in terms of certain topics of special interest to students.

* *Harvard Guide to American History*. Cambridge, Mass.: Harvard University Press, 1974. Oscar Handlin et al., eds.

Index to the Writings on American History. 1902–1940. Washington, D.C.: American Historical Association, 1956.

* *American Historical Association: A Guide to Historical Literature*. New York: Macmillan, 1961. See chapter on United States history.

Bibliographies in American History: A Guide to Materials for Research. Paterson, N.J.: Pageant Books, 1959. This work covers up to 1942. Henry P. Beers, ed.

A Bibliography of American Autobiographies. Madison: University of Wisconsin Press, 1961. Louis Kaplan et al. An important source if you are researching the life of a historical figure.

Dictionary of American History. New York: Scribners, 1940. James T. Adams and Roy V. Coleman, eds.

* *Concise Dictionary of American History.* New York: Scribners, 1962. Thomas C. Cochran and Wayne Andrews, eds.

Literary History of the United States: Bibliography. New York: Macmillan, 1948. Robert E. Spiller et al., eds. This is an important source for historical studies of literature.

U.S.-iana, 1650–1950: A Selective Bibliography. New York: Bowker, 1962. Wright Howes, ed.

American Social History Since 1860. New York: Appleton Century Crofts, 1970. Robert H. Bremner.

American Social History Before 1860. New York: Appleton Century Crofts, 1970. Gerald N. Grob.

* *Encyclopedia of American History.* New York: Harper & Row, 1970. Richard B. Morris, ed.

Historical Atlas of the United States. New York: Henry Holt, 1953. Clifford Lord and Elizabeth Lord, eds.

Our United States: Its History in Maps. Chicago: Denoyer-Geppert, 1956. Edgar B. Wesley, ed.

For sources on the United States government, see "United States Government Publications" on pages 92–93.

V. STATE, COUNTY, AND LOCAL UNITED STATES HISTORY

The Nature and Practice of Local History. Washington, D.C.: American Historical Association, 1958. Philip D. Jordan.

Bibliography of County Histories of the 3111 Counties in the United States. Baltimore: Clarence Peterson, 1946.

State Publications: A Provisional List of Official Publications of the Several States of the United States. New York: Publishers Weekly, 1908. Richard R. Bowker, ed.

The Official Publications of American Counties. Fort Collins, Colo.: 1937. James G. Hodgson.

* *Directory: Historical Societies and Agencies in the United States and Canada, 1973–74.* Nashville: American Association for State and Local History, 1972. Donna McDonald, ed.

W. REGIONAL UNITED STATES HISTORY

* *American Historical Association: Guide to Historical Literature.* New York: Macmillan, 1961. Chapter on United States History is broken down regionally.
* *Harvard Guide to American History.* Cambridge, Mass.: Harvard University Press, 1974. Oscar Handlin et al., eds. Sources are broken down according to both regions and periods.

X. UNITED STATES DIPLOMATIC HISTORY

Guide to the Diplomatic History of the United States, 1775–1921. Washington, D.C.: Government Printing Office, 1935. Samuel F. Bemis and Grace G. Griffin, eds.

Index to United States Documents Relating to Foreign Affairs, 1828–1861. Washington, D.C.: Carnegie Institute, 1914–1921. Adelaide R. Hasse, ed.

Treaties and Other International Acts of the United States of America. Washington, D.C.: Government Printing Office, 1931–present. D. Hunter Miller, ed.

* *Foreign Affairs Bibliography: A Selected and Annotated List of Books on International Relations* [1919–present]. New York: Harper & Row, 1933, 1943, 1953 and R. R. Bowker, 1964. Vol. I covers 1919–1932; Vol. II, 1932–1942; Vol. III, 1942–1952; Vol. IV, 1952–1962.

* *Foreign Relations of the United States.* Washington, D.C.: Government Printing Office, 1861–present. United States Department of State. These volumes are issued annually and contain actual diplomatic correspondence. These are *primary* sources rather than bibliographies. They are listed because most libraries have them.

General Index to the Published Volumes of the Diplomatic Correspondence of the United States, 1861–1899. Washington, D.C.: Government Printing Office, 1902. United States Department of State.

A Bibliography of United States–Latin American Relations Since 1810. Lincoln: University of Nebraska Press, 1968. David F. Trask et al., eds.

Y. SPECIAL TOPICS IN UNITED STATES HISTORY

Labor History

Labor History in the United States: A General Bibliography.
Urbana: University of Illinois, Institute of Labor and
Industrial Relations, 1962. Gene S. Stroud and Gilbert
E. Donahue, eds.

*American Labor History in Journals of History: A Bibliog-
raphy.* Urbana: University of Illinois, Institute of Labor
and Industrial Relations, 1962. Fred D. Rose, ed.

Black History

A Bibliography of Antislavery in America. Ann Arbor: University of Michigan Press, 1961. Dwight L. Dumond, ed.

* *A Layman's Guide to Negro History.* New York: McGraw-
Hill, 1967. Erwin A. Salk, ed.

* *The Negro in America: A Bibliography.* Cambridge, Mass.:
Harvard University Press, 1970. Elizabeth W. Miller, comp.

* *A Bibliographic History of Blacks in America Since 1528.*
New York: McKay, 1971. Edgar A. Toppin.

The Negro in the United States: A Research Guide. Bloomington: University of Indiana Press, 1965. Erwin K.
Welsch.

* *Blacks in America: Bibliographical Essays.* New York: Dou-
bleday, 1971. James M. McPherson et al.

*Black History Viewpoints: A Selected Bibliographical Guide
to Resources for Afro-American and African History.* Westport, Conn.: African Bibliographic Center, 1969.

*Black Studies: A Bibliography for the Use of Schools, Libraries
and the General Reader.* Brooklawn, N.J.: McKinley, 1973.
Leonard B. Irwin, comp.

* *The Negro in the United States: A Selected Bibliography.*
Washington, D.C.: Library of Congress, 1970, and University Microfilms, 1969. Dorothy B. Porter, ed.

The American Negro Reference Book. Englewood Cliffs, N.J.:
Prentice-Hall, 1966. John P. Davis.

Mexican-American History

Mexican-American History: A Critical Selective Bibliography.

Santa Barbara, Cal.: Mexican-American Historical Society, 1969.

* *The Mexican American: A Selected and Annotated Bibliography.* Stanford: Stanford University Press, 1971. Luis G.
Nogales, ed.

Bibliografía de Aztlán: An Annotated Chicano Bibliography.
San Diego: San Diego State College, 1971. Ernie Barrios,
comp.

* *The Mexican American: A Selected and Annotated Bibliography.* Stanford: Stanford University Press, 1969, John
J. Johnson, ed.

*Mexican American: Resources to Build Cultural Understand-
ing.* Littleton, Colo.: Libraries Unlimited, 1973. Lois B.
Jordan.

Puerto Rican History

* *Puerto Ricans on the United States Mainland.* Totowa, N.J.:
Rowman and Littlefield, 1972. Francesco Cordasco, ed.

* *The Puerto Ricans: An Annotated Bibliography.* New York:
Bowker, 1973. Paquita Vivó, ed.

* *An Annotated, Selected Puerto Rican Bibliography.* New
York: Columbia University Press, 1972. Enrique R. Bravo,
comp.

The Puerto Ricans 1493–1973: A Chronology and Fact Book.
Dobbs Ferry, N.Y.: Oceana, 1973. Francesco Cordasco,
ed.

Bibliography of Puerto Ricans in the United States. New York:
Department of Labor, Commonwealth of Puerto Rico,
1959. Clarence Senior, ed.

*The Spanish Speaking in the United States: A Guide to Ma-
terials.* Washington, D.C.: Cabinet Commission on Oppor-
tunities for the Spanish Speaking, 1971.

Historical Dictionary of Puerto Rico and the Virgin Islands.
Metuchen, N.J.: Scarecrow Press, 1973. Kenneth Farr,
comp.

Women's History

*The American Woman in Colonial and Revolutionary Times,
1565–1800: A Syllabus with Bibliography.* Philadelphia:

University of Pennsylvania Press, 1962. Eurenie Leonard et al.

Women's Magazines, 1693–1968. London: Michael Joseph, 1970. Cynthia L. White, ed.

* *Index to Women of the World from Ancient to Modern Times.* Westwood, Mass.: Faxon, 1970. Norma O. Ireland.

* *Notable American Women, 1607–1950: A Bibliographical Dictionary.* Cambridge, Mass.: Harvard University Press, 1971. Edward T. James, ed.

Women: A Bibliography on their Education and Careers. Washington, D.C.: Human Services Press, 1971. Helen S. Astin et al., eds.

Immigrant and Ethnic History

The Minority Experience: A Basic Bibliography of American Ethnic Studies. Santa Rosa, Cal.: Sonoma County, Superintendent of Schools, 1970.

Encyclopedic Dictionary of Ethnic Newspapers and Periodicals in the United States. Littleton, Colo.: Libraries Unlimited, 1972. Lubomyr S. Wynar.

Italians in the United States: A Bibliography of Reports, Texts, Critical Studies and Related Materials. New York: Oriole Editions, 1972. Francesco Cordasco and Salvatore La Gumina.

Ethnic and Racial Minorities in America: A Selected Bibliography of the Geographical Literature. Monticello, Ill.: Council of Planning Librarians, 1973. John A. Jackle, ed.

The British in America 1578–1970: A Chronology and Fact Book. Dobbs Ferry, N.Y.: Oceana, 1972. Howard B. Furer, ed. Volume covers the English, Scotch, Welsh, and Scotch-Irish.

The Germans in America 1607–1970: A Chronology and Fact Book. Dobbs Ferry, N.Y.: Oceana, 1973. Howard B. Furer, ed.

The Scandinavians in America 986–1970: A Chronology and Fact Book. Dobbs Ferry, N.Y.: Oceana, 1972. Howard B. Furer, ed.

The Italians in America 1492–1970: A Chronology and Fact Book. Dobbs Ferry, N.Y.: Oceana, 1972. Anthony F. La Gatto, ed.

The Poles in America 1608–1970: A Chronology and Fact Book. Dobbs Ferry, N.Y.: Oceana, 1973. Frank Renkiewicz, ed.

The Dutch in America 1609–1970: A Chronology and Fact Book. Dobbs Ferry, N.Y.: Oceana, 1973. Frank Renkie-J. W. Smit, eds.

The Jews in America 1621–1970: A Chronology and Fact Book. Dobbs Ferry, N.Y.: Oceana, 1971. Irving J. Sloan, ed.

Hungarians in America: A Biographical Directory. Philadelphia: Alpha Publications, 1971. Desi K. Bognar, ed.

A Bibliographic Guide to Greeks in the United States, 1890–1968. New York: Center for Migration Studies, 1970. Michael N. Cutsumbis.

American Ethnic Groups: A Sourcebook for the 1970's. Mt. Pleasant, Iowa: Social Science and Sociological Resources, 1973. Jack Kinton, ed.

American Indian History

Handbook of American Indians North of Mexico. New York: Pageant, 1959. Frederick W. Hodge, et al.

* *The Indian Heritage of America.* New York: Knopf, 1968. Alvin M. Josephy, Jr. See bibliography at end of book.

Reference Encyclopedia of the American Indian. New York: B. Klein and Company, 1967, and Rye, N.Y.: Todd, 1973. Bernard Klein and Daniel Icolari, eds.

Index to Literature on the American Indian. n.p.: Indian Historian Press, 1972. American Indian Historical Society.

The American Indian 1492–1970: A Chronology and Fact Book. Dobbs Ferry, N.Y.: Oceana, 1971. Henry C. Dennis, ed.

Miscellaneous Topics

Guide to Business History. Cambridge, Mass.: Harvard University Press, 1948. Henrietta M. Larson.

A Critical Bibliography of Religion in America. Princeton: Princeton University Press, 1961. Nelson R. Burr, ed.

Encyclopedia of the American Revolution. New York: McKay, 1966. Mark M. Boatner.

Civil War Books: A Critical Bibliography. Baton Rouge:

Louisiana State University Press, 1967–1968. Allan Nevins, ed.

The Progressive Era and the Great War, 1896–1920. New York: Appleton Century Crofts, 1969. Arthur S. Link and William M. Leary, Jr., comps.

World War II: Books in English, 1945–1965. Stanford, Cal.: Hoover Institution, 1971. Janet Ziegler, comp.

The Civil War Dictionary. New York: David McKay, 1959. Mark M. Boatner.

8. SOURCES FOR HISTORICAL STATISTICS AND OTHER QUANTITATIVE DATA

Historical Tables, 58 B.C.–A.D. 1955. New York: St. Martin's Press, 1956. Sigfrid H. Steinberg.

Bibliography of Selected Statistical Sources on the American Nations. Washington, D.C.: Inter-American Statistical Institute, 1947.

Historical Statistics of the United States, Colonial Times to 1957. Washington, D.C.: Bureau of the Census, 1960.

* Statistical Abstract of the United States. Washington, D.C.: Government Printing Office, 1878–present. Annual.

A Report on World Population Migrations as Related to the United States. Washington, D.C.: George Washington University, 1956.

Statistical Yearbooks: An Annotated Bibliography of the General Statistical Yearbooks of Major Political Subdivisions of the World. Washington, D.C.: 1953.

Demographic Yearbook. New York: United Nations, Statistical Office, 1949–present. Annual.

Population Index. Princeton: Office of Population Research, 1935–present.

9. GUIDES TO PHOTOCOPIED AND NONPRINTED SOURCES

American Historical Association Guide to Photocopied Historical Materials in the United States and Canada. Ithaca: Cornell University Press, 1961. Richard W. Hale, ed.

Union List of Microfilms. Ann Arbor: J. W. Edwards, 1951. Eleanor E. Campion, comp.

List of National Archives Microfilm Publications. Washington,
D.C.: National Archives and Records Service, 1961.

Subject Guide to Microfilms in Print. Washington, D.C.: Microcard Editions, 1962–present. Albert J. Diaz, ed.

*Guide to the Special Collections of Prints and Photographs in
the Library of Congress.* Washington, D.C.: Government
Printing Office, 1955. Paul Vanderbilt, ed.

Library of Congress Catalogue: Motion Pictures and Filmstrips. Washington, D.C.: Library of Congress, 1953–
present. Annual.

Library of Congress Catalogue: Music and Phonorecords.
Washington, D.C.: Library of Congress, 1953–present.
Annual.

Picture Sources: An Introductory List. New York: Special
Libraries Association, 1959. Helen Faye, ed.

The Oral History Collection of Columbia University. New
York: Columbia University Oral History Research Office,
1964.

Oral History in the United States: A Directory. New York:
Oral History Association, 1971. Gary L. Shumway, comp.
Locates and describes oral history collections.

10. GUIDES TO ABSTRACTS, ARCHIVES, DISSERTATIONS, AND CURRENT RESEARCH

Dissertation Abstracts: Abstracts of Dissertations and Monographs in Microfilm. Ann Arbor: University Microfilms,
1961.

A Guide to Archives and Manuscripts in the United States.
New Haven, Conn.: Yale University Press, 1961. Philip
C. Hamer, ed.

The National Union Catalog of Manuscript Collections. Ann
Arbor: J. W. Edwards, 1962. Library of Congress Catalogue.

appendix B

Useful Information for the Historian

State Historical Societies

If your topic concerns the history of a particular state, one of the best sources of information is the state historical societies. These groups maintain archives, do research, publish journals, and do many other tasks concerning the histories of their states. They can also help you locate information on county and local history. By writing to or visiting these societies you can find out if books or archives on state or local history are located near enough to your school to be useful as part of your research. Access to archival materials can make history research very exciting. Most towns, especially if they are county seats (the town in which county governments are located) keep local and county records, many of which may be available to the public. If your school or home is located in a large city, there will likely be one or more private or city historical societies.

If you desire information on state or local history and you are aware of no source close by, contact the appropriate state historical society.

Alabama Historical Association, 3121 Carlisle Road, Birmingham, 35213.

Arizona Historical Society, 949 East 2nd Street, Tucson, 85719.

Arkansas Historical Association, History Department, University of Arkansas, Fayetteville, 71703.

California Historical Society, 2090 Jackson Street, San Francisco, 94115.

State Historical Society of Colorado, 200 Fourteenth Avenue, Denver, 80203.

Connecticut Historical Society, 1 Elizabeth Street, Hartford, 06105.

Historical Society of Delaware, 505 Market Street, Wilmington, 19801.

Florida Historical Society, University of South Florida Library, Tampa, 33620.

Georgia Historical Commission, 116 Mitchell Street, S.W., Atlanta, 30303.

Hawaiian Historical Society, 560 Kawaiahao Street, Honolulu, 96813.

Idaho State Historical Society, 610 N. Julia Davis Drive, Boise, 83706.

Illinois State Historical Society, Old State Capitol Building, Springfield, 62706.

Indiana Historical Bureau, State Library and History Building, Indianapolis, 46204.

Iowa State Department of History and Archives, East 12th Street and Grand Avenue, Des Moines, 50319.

Kansas State Historical Society, Memorial Building, 120 West 10th Street, Topeka, 66612.

Kentucky Historical Society, Box H, Frankfort, 40601.

Louisiana Historical Association, Box 44422, Capitol Station, Baton Rouge, 70804.

Maine Historical Society, 487 Congress Street, Portland, 04111.

Maryland Historical Society, 201 West Monument Street at Park Avenue, Baltimore, 21202.

Massachusetts Historical Society, 1154 Boylston Street, Boston, 02215.

Historical Society of Michigan, 2117 Washtenaw Avenue, Ann Arbor, 48104.

Minnesota Historical Society, 690 Cedar Street, St. Paul, 55101.

Mississippi Historical Society, Box 571, Jackson, 39205.

Missouri Historical Society, Jefferson Memorial Building, St. Louis, 63112.

Montana Historical Society, 225 North Roberts Street, Helena, 59601.

Nebraska State Historical Society, 1500 R Street, Lincoln, 68508.

New Hampshire Historical Society, 30 Park Street, Concord, 03301.

New Jersey Historical Commission, State Library, 185 West State Street, Trenton, 08625.

Historical Society of New Mexico, Box 1442, Socorro, 87801.

New York Historical Society, 170 Central Park West, New York 10024.

North Carolina State Department of Archives and History, 109 East Jones Street, Raleigh, 27602.

State Historical Society of North Dakota, Liberty Memorial Building, Bismarck, 58501.

Ohio Historical Society, Ohio Historical Center, Columbus, 43211.

Oklahoma Historical Society, Historical Building, Oklahoma City, 73105.

Oregon Historical Society, 1230 S.W. Park Avenue, Portland, 97205.

Pennsylvania Historical and Museum Commission, Box 1026, Harrisburg, 17108.

Rhode Island Historical Society, 52 Power Street, Providence, 02906.

South Carolina Department of Archives and History, 1430 Senate Street, Columbus, 29211.

South Dakota State Historical Society, Soldiers and Sailors Memorial Building, Pierre, 57501.

Tennessee Historical Commission, 403 Seventh Avenue, North Nashville, 37219.

Texas Library and Historical Commission, 1201 Brazos, Box
12927 Capitol Station, Austin, 78711.
Utah State Historical Society, 603 E. South Temple, Salt Lake
City, 84102.
Vermont Historical Society, Pavilion Building, Montpelier,
05602.
Virginia Historical Society, 428 North Boulevard, Richmond,
23221.
Washington State Historical Society, 315 North Stadium Way,
Tacoma, 98403.
West Virginia Department of Archives and History, 400 East
Wing, State Capitol, Charleston, 25305.
State Historical Society of Wisconsin, 816 State Street, Madison, 53706.
Wyoming State Archives and History Department, State Office
Building, Cheyenne, 82001.

Research and Study Guides in History

If you wish to consult a history study guide written for
more advanced students, here is a list of some recent publications.

Wood Gray, *Historian's Handbook: A Key to the Study and
Writing of History.* Boston: Houghton Mifflin, 1964.
Norman Cantor and Richard Schneider, *How to Study History.*
New York: T. Y. Crowell, 1967.
Robert Daniels, *Studying History: How and Why.* Englewood
Cliffs, N.J.: Prentice-Hall, 1972.
Robert Shafer, *A Guide to Historical Method.* Homewood,
Ill.: Dorsey, 1974.

Grammar and Style Manuals

If you know that your background in grammar and composition is weak, or if you need more specific information concerning report writing, here are a few manuals that should
help.

Jacques Barzun and Henry Graff, *The Modern Researcher.*
New York: Harcourt, 1970.

Cecil B. Williams, *A Research Manual for College Studies and Papers.* New York: Harper & Row, 1963.

University of Chicago Press, *A Manual of Style.* Chicago: University of Chicago Press, 1969.

Kate L. Turabian, *A Manual for Writers of Term Papers, Theses, and Dissertations.* Chicago: University of Chicago Press, 1973.

Call Numbers: The Library of Congress System

The identification system of the Library of Congress divides the major subject classifications by letter. The following are the Library of Congress subject categories and their respective letter designations.

A   General works
B   Philosophy, psychology, religion
C   Auxiliary sciences of history
D   General and Old World history
E   American (Western Hemisphere) history
F   American history (continued)
G   Geography, anthropology, customs, sports
H   Social sciences, economics, socialism
J   Political science, international law
K   Law
L   Education
M   Music
N   Fine arts
P   Language, literature
Q   Science
R   Medicine
S   Agriculture
T   Technology
U   Military science
V   Naval science
Z   Bibliography, library science

Each letter group is broken down further by the addition of a second letter and then by numbers. Here are some of the breakdowns of the categories D, E, and F, which deal with history.

D	General history
DA	Great Britain
	20–690 England
	700–745 Wales
	750–890 Scotland
	900–995 Ireland
DB	Austria-Hungary
DC	France
DD	Germany
DE	Classical antiquity
DF	Greece
DG	Italy
DH-DJ	Netherlands
	DH 1–207 Belgium and Holland
	DH 401–811 Belgium
	DH 901–925 Luxemburg (grand duchy)
	DJ Holland
DK	Russia
	1–272 Russia (general)
	401–441 Poland
	445–465 Finland
	750–891 Russia in Asia
DL	Scandinavia
	1– 85 Scandinavia (general)
	101–291 Denmark
	301–398 Iceland
	401–596 Norway
	601–991 Sweden
DP	Spain and Portugal
	1–402 Spain
	501–900 Portugal
DQ	Switzerland
DR	Turkey and the Balkan States
DS	Asia
DT	Africa
DU	Australia and Oceania
DX	Gypsies

E America (General) and United States (General)
      11–143 America (general)

31– 45 North America (general)
51– 99 Indians of North America
101–135 Discovery of America
151–810 United States
151–185 General history and description
185 Negroes in the United States
186–199 Colonial period
201–298 Revolution
351–364 War of 1812
401–415 War with Mexico
441–453 Slavery
458–655 Civil War
482–489 Confederate States
714–735 War with Spain

F   United States (local) and America except the United States

1– 970 United States (local)
1001–1140 British North America, Canada, Newfoundland
1201–1392 Mexico
1401–1419 Latin America (general)
1421–1577 Central America
1601–2151 West Indies
2201–2239 South America (general)
2251–2299 Colombia
2301–2349 Venezuela
2351–2471 Guiana: British, Dutch, French
2501–2659 Brazil
2661–2699 Paraguay
2701–2799 Uruguay
2801–3021 Argentine Republic
3051–3285 Chile
3301–3359 Bolivia
3401–3619 Peru
3701–3799 Ecuador

Thus a volume whose call number begins DK 408 deals with Polish history, and one which begins E 451 is about the history of slavery in the United States.

Call Numbers: *The Dewey Decimal System*

The Dewey system is a decimal system. There are ten main subject headings, each containing 100 different numbers:

000–099	General works
100–199	Philosophy
200–299	Religion
300–399	Social sciences
400–499	Language
500–599	Pure science
600–699	Technology
700–799	The arts
800–899	Literature
900–999	History

Each of the main subject divisions is itself divided into ten sections of ten units each. The divisions of history are:

900–909	General history
910–919	Geography, travel, description
920–929	Biography
930–939	Ancient history
940–949	European history
950–959	Asian history
960–969	African history
970–979	North American history
980–989	South American history
990–999	Other regions of the world

Each of these divisions is further divided into ten parts. The divisions of 970 to 979 (North American history), for example, are as follows:

970	General North American history
971	Canadian history
972	Mexican and Caribbean history
973	General United States history
974	Northeastern states, U.S.
975	Southeastern states, U.S.
976	South-central states, U.S.
977	North-central states, U.S.
978	Western states, U.S.
979	Far-western states, U.S. and Alaska

Thus a volume whose call number begins with 934 deals with ancient history, and one that begins with 978 is concerned with the history of one or more of the western states of the United States.

Common Abbreviations Used in Footnotes, Bibliographies, Catalogs, and Reference Books

anon.	anonymous
app.	appendix
art.	article (plural, arts.)
b.	born
bk.	book (plural, bks.)
bull.	bulletin
c.	copyright
ca.	*circa*, about, approximately. Used with approximate dates, e.g., "ca. 1804."
cf.	*confer*, compare. Used only when the writer wishes the reader to compare two or more works.
ch. or chap.	chapter (plural, chaps.)
col.	column (plural, cols.)
comp.	compiler (plural, comps.)
d.	died
diss.	dissertation
e.g.	*exempli gratia*, for example
ed.	edition, editor (plural, eds.)
enl.	enlarged
et al.	*et alii*, and others
et seq.	*et sequens*, and the following
fac.	facsimile
fig.	figure (plural, figs.)
ibid.	*ibidem*, in the same place
id.	*idem*, the same (person)
i.e.	*id est*, that is
ill.	illustrated, illustration
infra.	below (referring to a later point in the work)
l. or ll.	line(s)

loc. cit.	*loco citato*, in the place cited (referring to the same passage cited in an immediately previous footnote)
MS	manuscript (plural, MSS)
n.	note, footnote (plural, nn.)
n.d.	no date (of publication is given)
n.p.	no place (of publication) or no publisher (is given)
no.	number (plural, nos.)
n.s.	new series
o.p.	out of print
op. cit.	*opere citato*, in the work cited
o.s.	old series
p.	page (plural, pp.)
par.	paragraph (plural, pars.)
passim	here and there (throughout the work cited)
pseud.	pseudonym
pt.	part (plural, pts.)
q.v.	*quod vide*, which see
rev.	revised
sc.	scene
sic	so, thus (Enclosed in brackets to indicate an error or unusual statement in a quotation.)
supp.	supplement (plural, supps.)
supra	above (referring to an earlier point in the work)
trans.	translator
v.	verse (plural, vv.)
viz.	*videlicet*, namely
vol.	volume, (plural, vols.)
vs.	*versus*, against